# Paint by Numbers

## Coloring Pixel & Areas Book

# *Volume 2*

# Smart Things Begin With Griddlers.net

Paint by Numbers - Coloring Pixel & Areas Book (Volume 2)

Published by: Griddlers.net
a division of A.A.H.R. Offset Maor Ltd

Author: Griddlers Team
Compiler: Shirly Maor
Cover design: Elad Maor
Cover background elements by: freepic
Contributors: abrek, Agrippina, Amyflemming, animgirl, arcadedweller, arkiteta, banane4joy, benjy_t, bepklep, beren2005, bingo7, cactus_fanatic, Calvario, carootje, chefmomster2, dado, dawgmind, debbbi, DinaGreen, dr_serdar, elimaor, ElinaMaria, eMJee, evengroen, f1comp, federicat83, GICaesar, Glucklich, goshenmike, hibrahimozer, inbarabc, ini, jatabe, jule, JynxsMom, kendrasong, kikiki, ledka, liri748, llamaluva, Makarios, maristone, marlonbraga, MDE001, meszi, mustafademirbas, myamollytaz, Mzzah, nasa17, netty, Nicky, popkin, replica, sandyeggan, sciguy, solior, som, starch, stephanieke159, strunka, stumpy, tbs, throwaway11, Turquoise, Unoalquadrato, vivimagi, vonnizen, wek82689, wiggles, wiklin, willem, wink5, xitvono, xxLadyJxx, yawetag, yeu, ZajberZ, Zlask, zz89.

ISBN: 978-9657679203

More information:
Email – team@griddlers.net
Website – http://www.griddlers.net

# About Paint by Numbers

These coloring pictures are made of original griddlers puzzles.

Though the puzzles themselves requires logic to solve them, the

results are always very nice images. For those of you who prefer

to relax when solving puzzles we decided to convert these nice

images into a coloring book.

There are color names under each puzzle which can sometimes

seem strange, however you can find colors by names on the back

cover of this book. This palette comes from a popular set of

colors. You can use any similar color.

**1-Black, 2-Yellow-Orange, 3-Timberwolf, 4-Fuzzy Wuzzy, 5-Sunset Orange**

**Dachshund**

**Nicky**

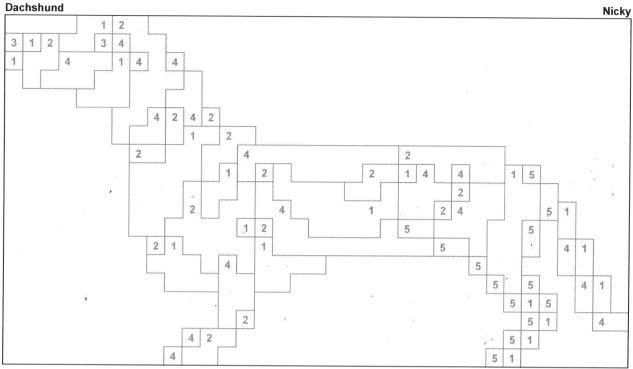

1-Brown, 2-Yellow-Orange, 3-Black, 4-Raw Sienna, 5-Tan

**Blue Street**

**evengroen**

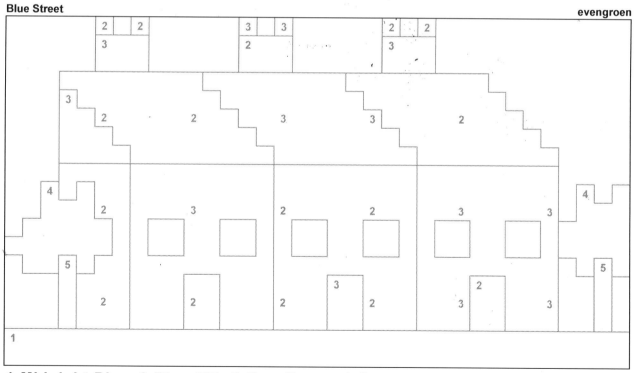

1-Midnight Blue, 2-Blue (III), 3-Cornflower, 4-Green, 5-Mango Tango

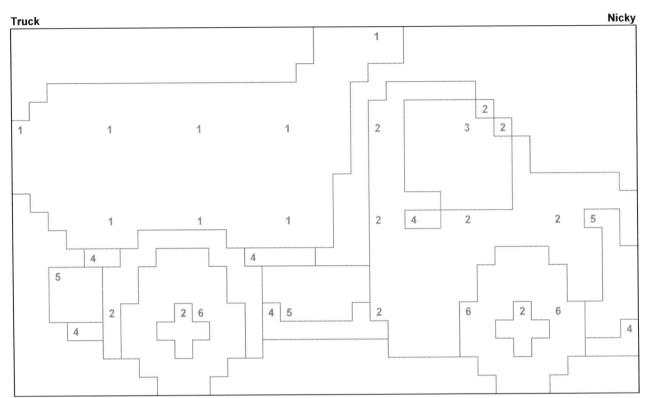

1-Shadow, 2-Yellow-Orange, 3-Timberwolf, 4-Outer Space, 5-Blue-Violet, 6-Black

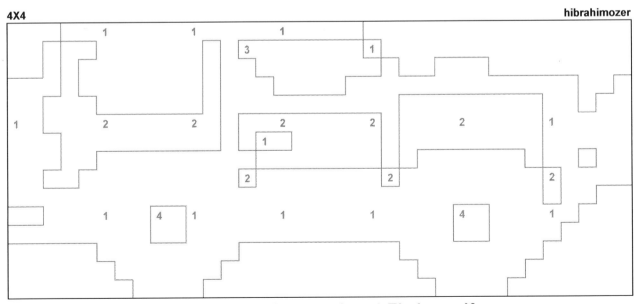

1-Black, 2-Granny Smith Apple, 3-Aquamarine, 4-Timberwolf

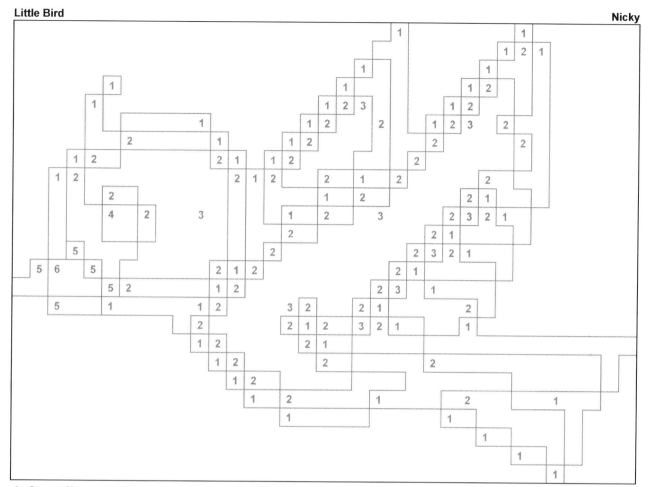

**1-Cornflower, 2-Aquamarine, 3-Timberwolf, 4-Black, 5-Macaroni and Cheese, 6 -Peach**

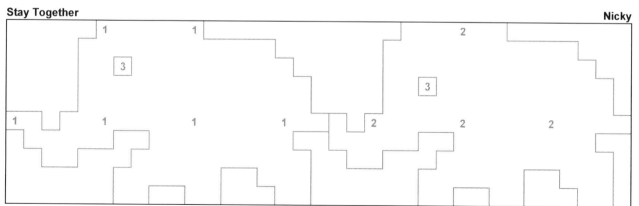

**1-Vivid Violet, 2-Manatee, 3-Outer Space**

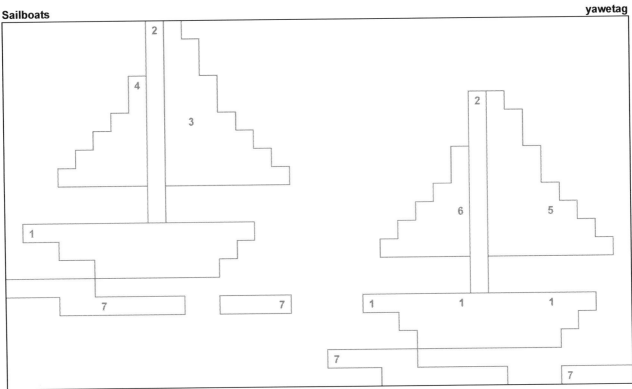

**1-Mahogany, 2-Cadet Blue, 3-Indigo, 4-Dandelion, 5-Asparagus, 6-Tan, 7-Pe riwinkle**

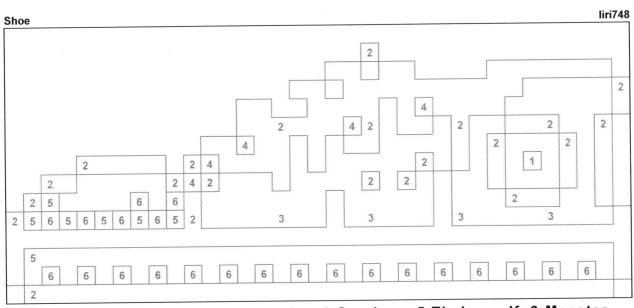

**1-Maroon, 2-Black, 3-Wild Blue Yonder, 4-Cerulean, 5-Timberwolf, 6-Manatee**

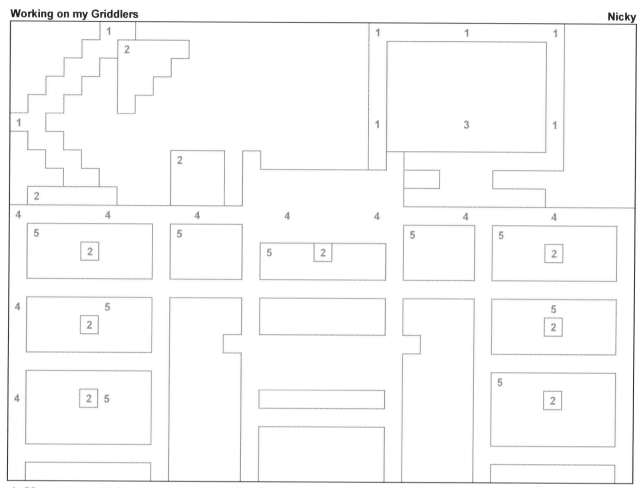

1-Manatee, 2-Asparagus, 3-Black, 4-Fuzzy Wuzzy, 5-Mango Tango

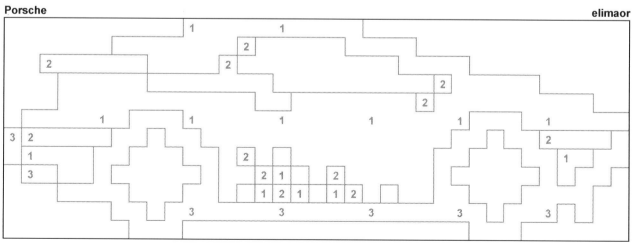

1-Scarlet, 2-Fuzzy Wuzzy, 3-Black

**Eye of the Tiger** — marlonbraga

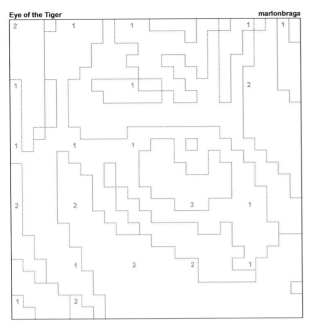

1-Black, 2-Mango Tango, 3-Inchworm

**Teddy Bear** — stumpy

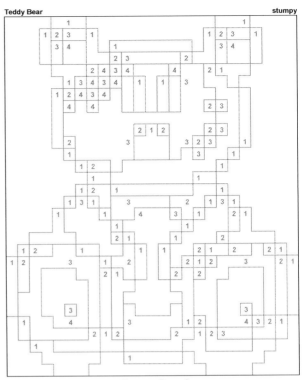

1-Black, 2-Beaver, 3-Tan, 4-Peach

**Eggplants** — federicat83

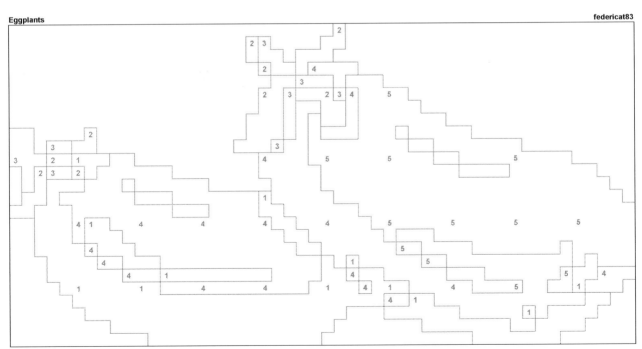

1-Eggplant, 2-Fern, 3-Asparagus, 4-Jazzberry Jam, 5-Cerise

**Flamingo**                                                    **Nicky**

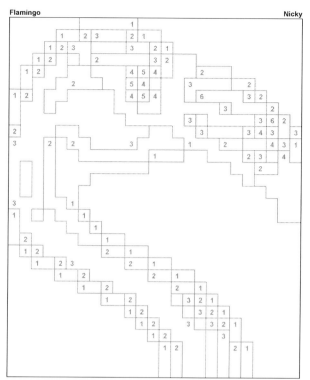

1-Brick Red, 2-Sunset Orange, 3-Bittersweet, 4-Black,
5-Eggplant, 6-Cotton Candy

**Rabbit**                                                      **Nicky**

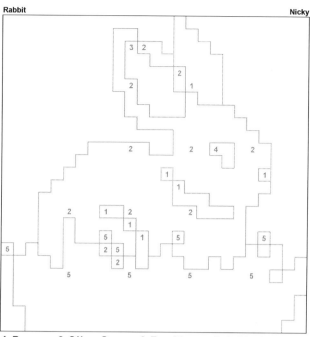

1-Beaver, 2-Olive Green, 3-Tumbleweed, 4-Black, 5-G
reen

**Goose**                                                    **DinaGreen**

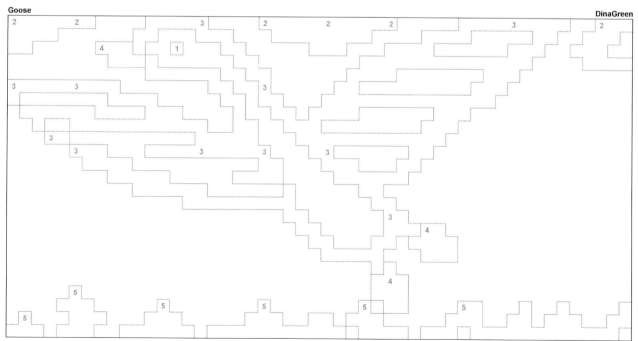

1-Black, 2-Cornflower, 3-Manatee, 4-Mango Tango, 5-Tropical Rain Forest

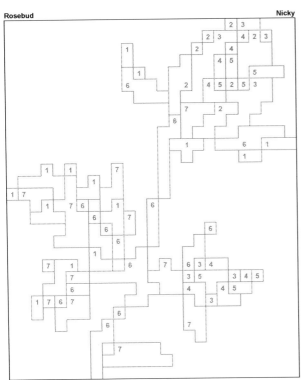

Rosebud — Nicky

1-Yellow-Green, 2-Mahogany, 3-Red, 4-Salmon, 5-Pig
Pink, 6-Tropical Rain Forest, 7-Green

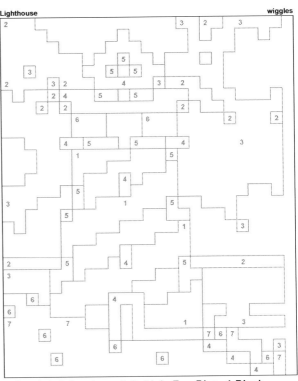

Lighthouse — wiggles

1-Scarlet, 2-Cerulean, 3-Robin's Egg Blue, 4-Black,
5-Manatee, 6-Mango Tango, 7-Tropical Rain Forest

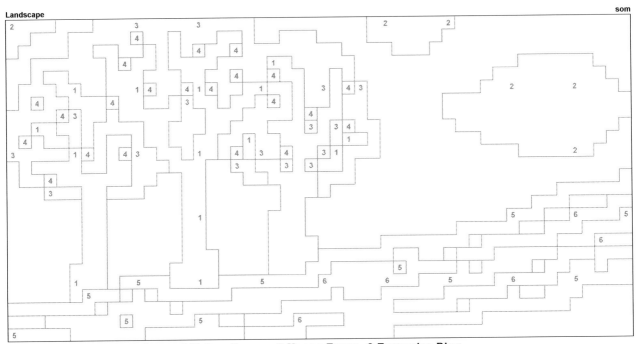

Landscape — som

1-Black, 2-Periwinkle, 3-Green, 4-Yellow-Orange, 5-Mango Tango, 6-Turquoise Blue

**Rose** abrek

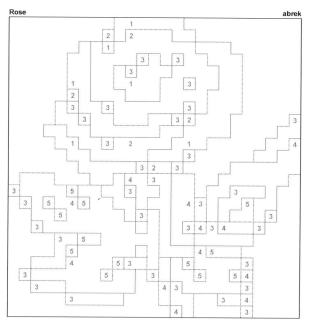

1-Scarlet, 2-Fuzzy Wuzzy, 3-Black, 4-Tropical Rain
Forest, 5-Green

**Cute Rabbit** meszi

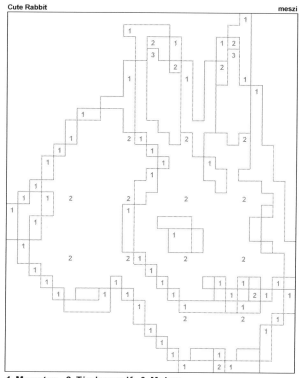

1-Manatee, 2-Timberwolf, 3-Melon

**Bookworm** elimaor

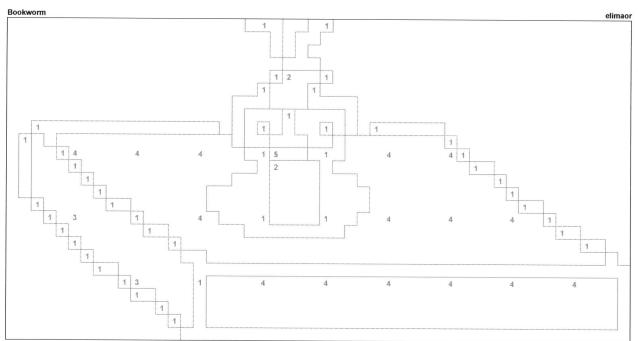

1-Black, 2-Green, 3-Banana Mania, 4-Plum, 5-Scarlet

**Brown Bird**                                              **Nicky**

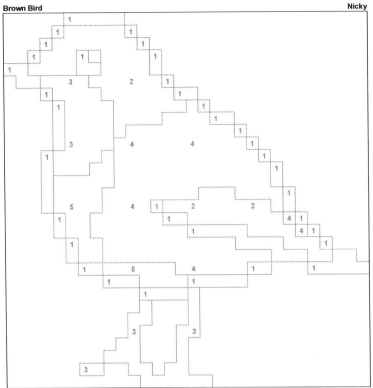

1-Black, 2-Fuzzy Wuzzy, 3-Mahogany, 4-Olive Green, 5-Shadow

**Squirrel**                                                **meszi**

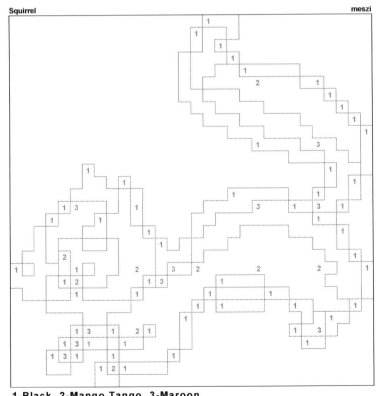

1-Black, 2-Mango Tango, 3-Maroon

Horse                                                                    arkiteta

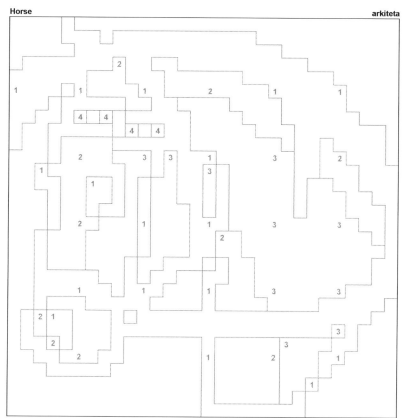

1-Black, 2-Fuzzy Wuzzy, 3-Mahogany, 4-Tropical Rain Forest

Hummingbird                                                              xitvono

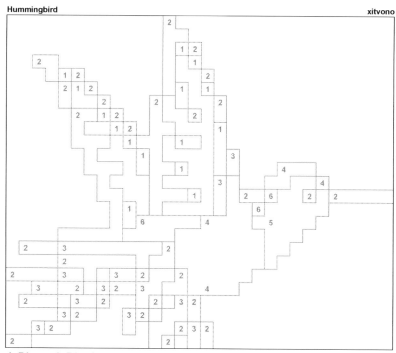

1-Plum, 2-Black, 3-Navy Blue, 4-Purple Heart, 5-Green, 6-Fuzzy
Wuzzy

**Cake**                                    Nicky

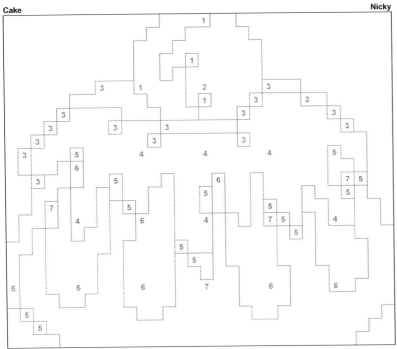

1-Indian Red, 2-Sunset Orange, 3-Yellow-Orange, 4-Yellow, 5-Outer Space, 6-Tan, 7-Fuzzy Wuzzy

**Butterfly**                              mustafademirbas

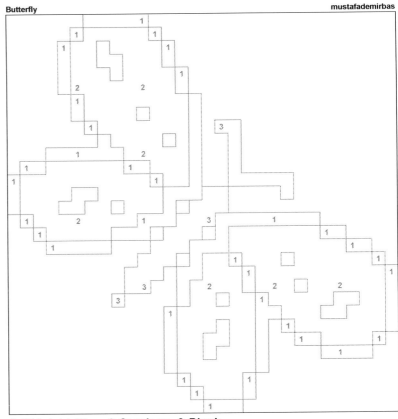

1-Midnight Blue, 2-Cerulean, 3-Black

**Monkey Wrench**

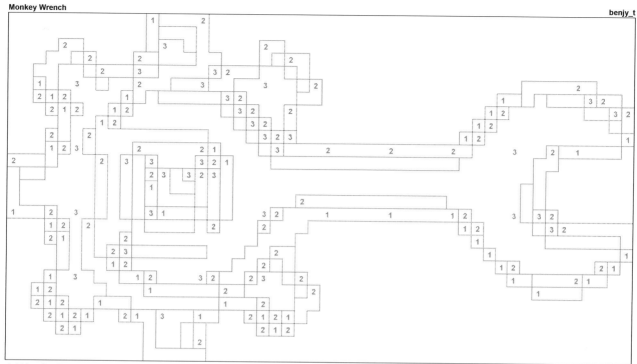

1-Black, 2-Manatee, 3-Periwinkle

**Turtle**

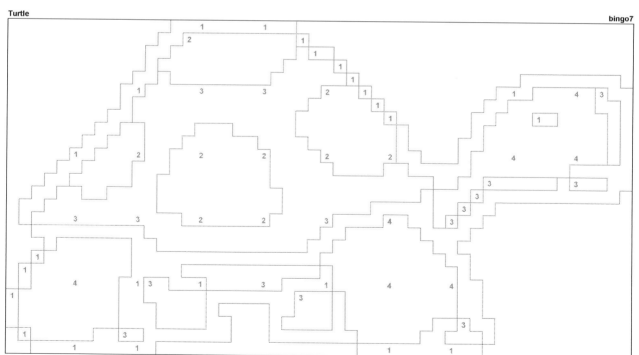

1-Black, 2-Fuzzy Wuzzy, 3-Shadow, 4-Olive Green

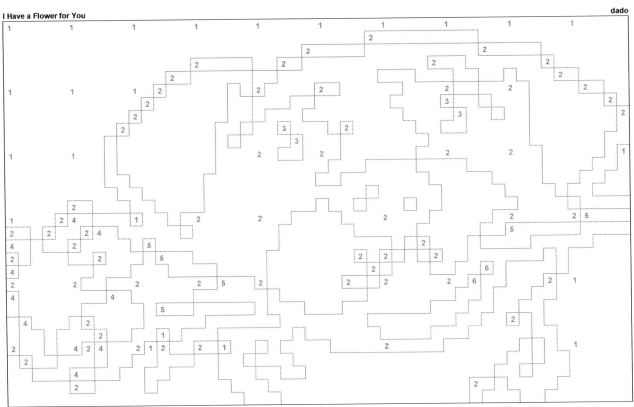

1-Cadet Blue, 2-Black, 3-Brown, 4-Dandelion, 5-Caribbean Green, 6-Scarlet

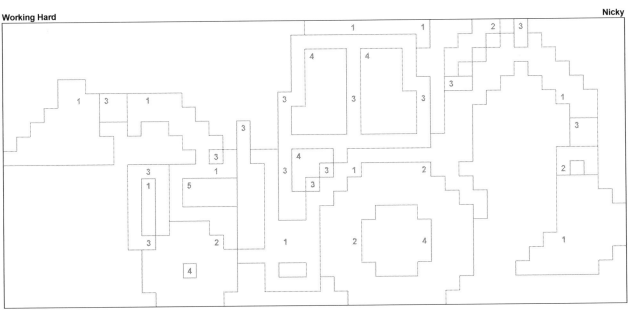

1-Dandelion, 2-Black, 3-Manatee, 4-Periwinkle, 5-Mahogany

**Rose**　　　　　　　　　　　　　　　　　　　　　　　　**Nicky**

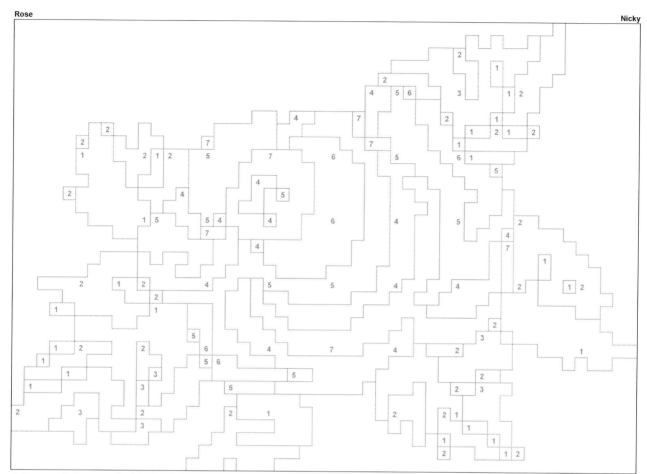

1-Green, 2-Granny Smith Apple, 3-Spring Green, 4-Blush, 5-Red-Violet, 6-Pig Pink, 7-Jazzberry Jam

**Snail**　　　　　　　　　　　　　　　　　　　　　　　　**starch**

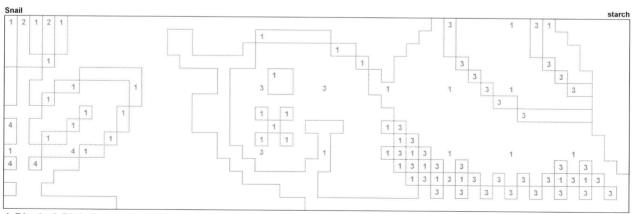

1-Black, 2-Pink Flamingo, 3-Yellow-Orange, 4-Granny Smith Apple

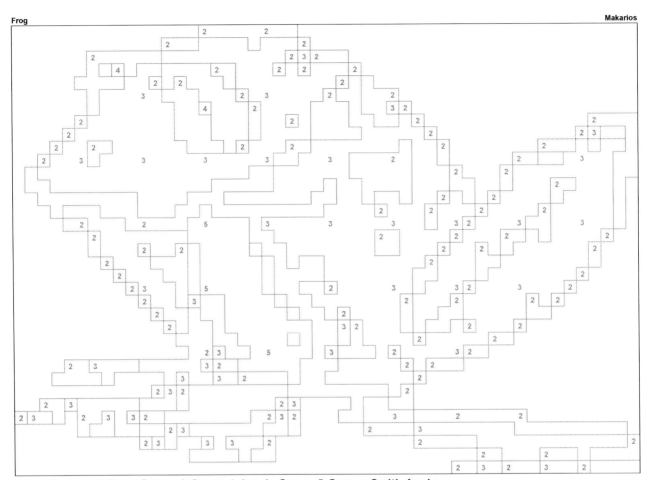

1-Red-Orange, 2-Outer Space, 3-Green, 4-Jungle Green, 5-Granny Smith Apple

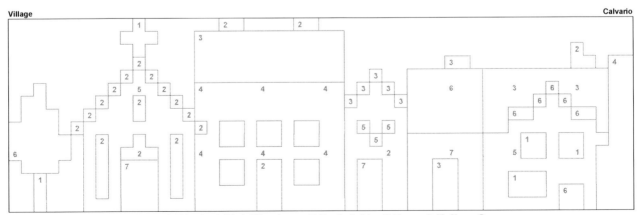

1-Mango Tango, 2-Cerulean, 3-Black, 4-Pink Flamingo, 5-Periwinkle, 6-Fern, 7-Yellow-Orange

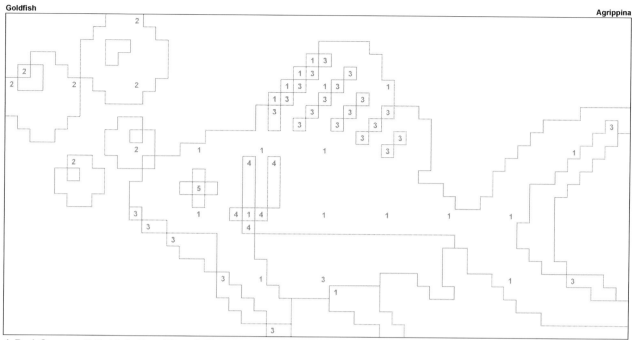

1-Red-Orange, 2-Robin's Egg Blue, 3-Macaroni and Cheese, 4-Mango Tango, 5-Black

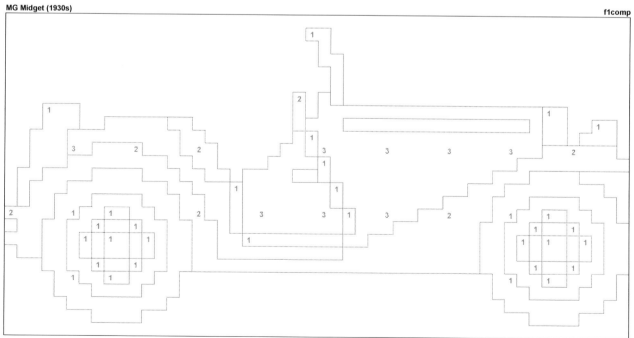

1-Manatee, 2-Black, 3-Wild Blue Yonder

1-Black, 2-Wild Strawberry, 3-Purple Heart, 4-Yellow-Orange

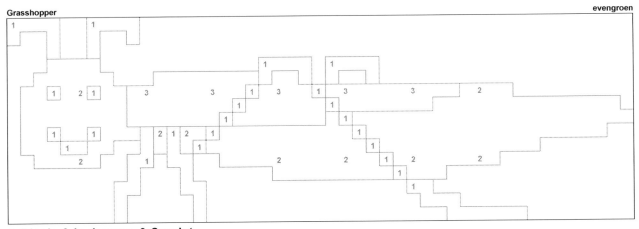

1-Black, 2-Inchworm, 3-Scarlet

Fan

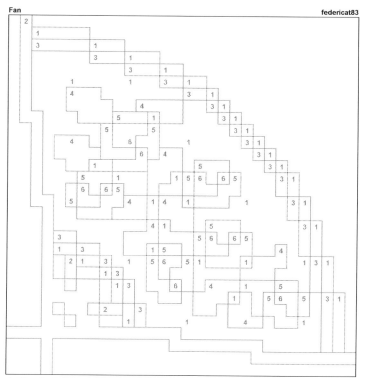

1-Black, 2-Fuzzy Wuzzy, 3-Yellow, 4-Green, 5-Pig Pink, 6-Magenta

Lego

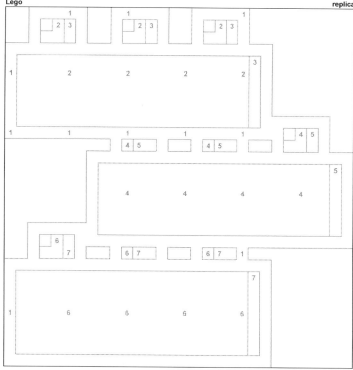

1-Black, 2-Denim, 3-Midnight Blue, 4-Dandelion, 5-Inchworm,
6-Scarlet, 7-Jazzberry Jam

**Toucan**                                                    **cactus_fanatic**

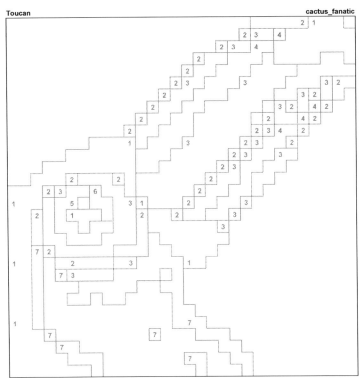

1-Black, 2-Red-Orange, 3-Yellow-Orange, 4-Peach, 5-Robin's Egg
Blue, 6-Cornflower, 7-Timberwolf

**Orange Atmosphere**                                          **elimaor**

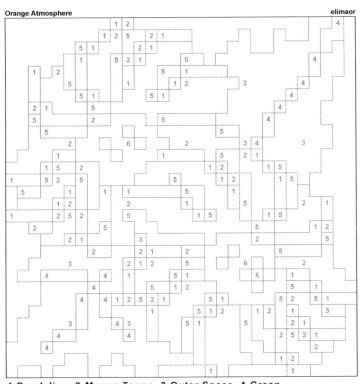

1-Dandelion, 2-Mango Tango, 3-Outer Space, 4-Green,
5-Red-Orange, 6-Fuzzy Wuzzy

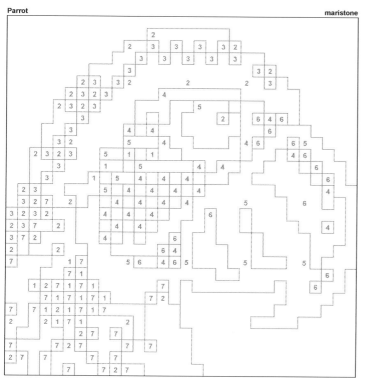

1-Goldenrod, 2-Denim, 3-Turquoise Blue, 4-Cadet Blue, 5-Black,
6-Manatee, 7-Asparagus

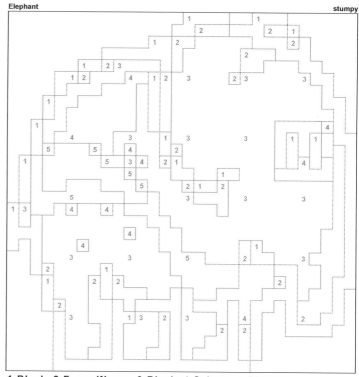

1-Black, 2-Fuzzy Wuzzy, 3-Blush, 4-Salmon, 5-Pig Pink

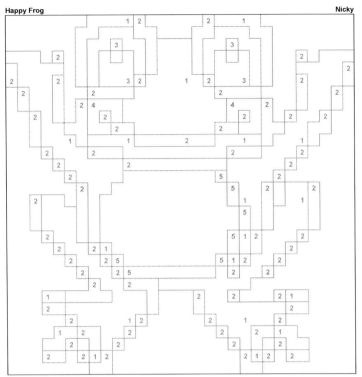

1-Inchworm, 2-Yellow-Green, 3-Black, 4-Magenta, 5-Tropical Rain Forest

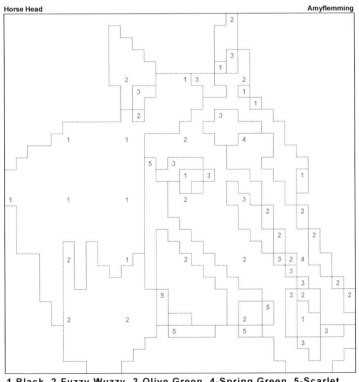

1-Black, 2-Fuzzy Wuzzy, 3-Olive Green, 4-Spring Green, 5-Scarlet

**Basket**

nasa17

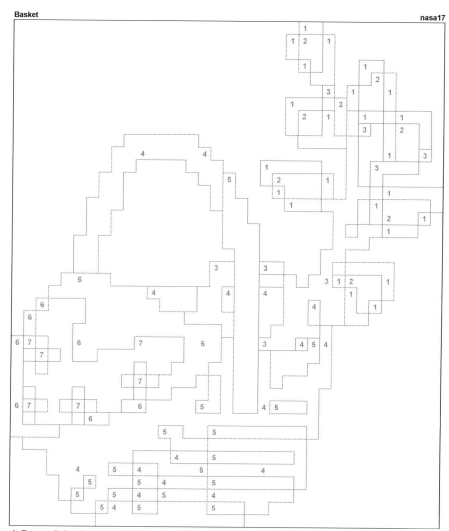

1-Fern, 2-Inchworm, 3-Green, 4-Eggplant, 5-Indian Red, 6-Brick Red, 7-Bittersweet

**Renault F1**

f1comp

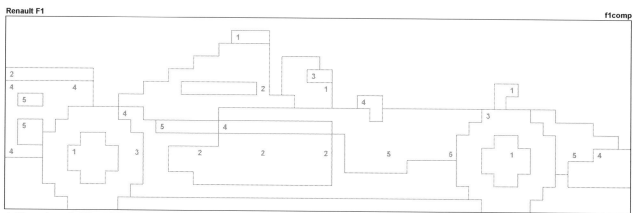

1-Manatee, 2-Blue (III), 3-Black, 4-Midnight Blue, 5-Dandelion

**Koala**                                                          **Nicky**

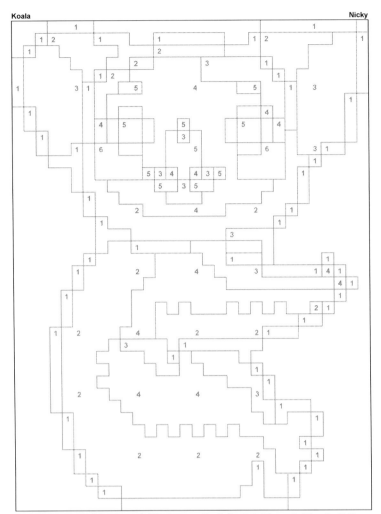

1-Eggplant, 2-Shadow, 3-Timberwolf, 4-Cadet Blue, 5-Black, 6-B
lush

**Ducks in a Row**                                                **animgirl**

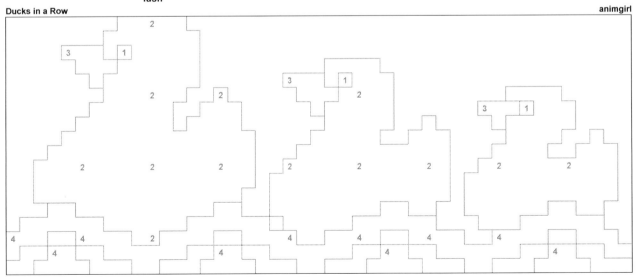

1-Black, 2-Dandelion, 3-Mango Tango, 4-Green-Blue

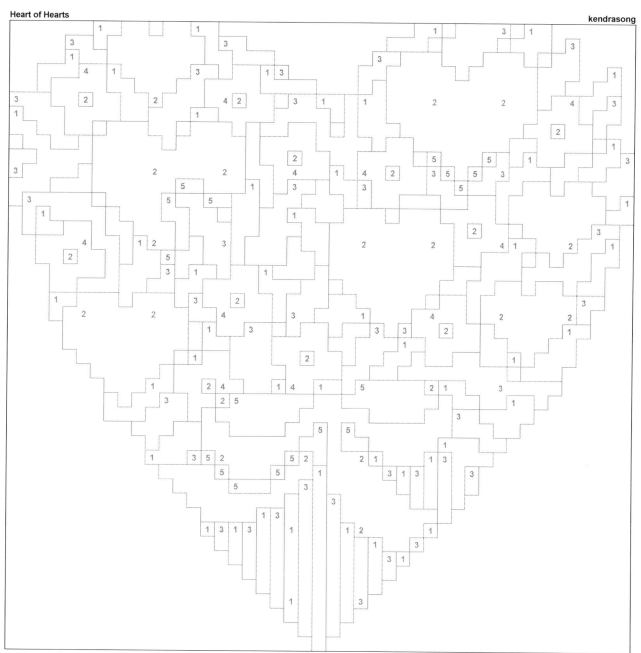

1-Outer Space, 2-Maroon, 3-Asparagus, 4-Desert Sand, 5-Eggplant

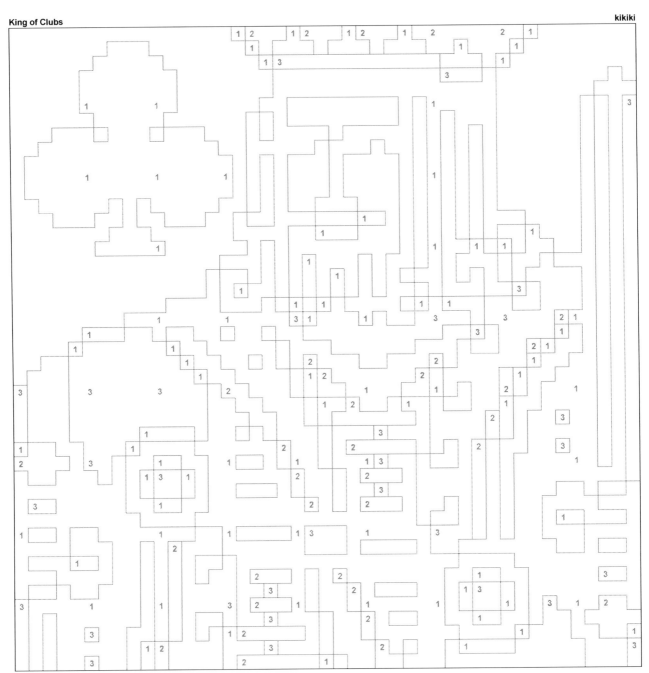

1-Black, 2-Dandelion, 3-Scarlet

Fuchsia

Makarios

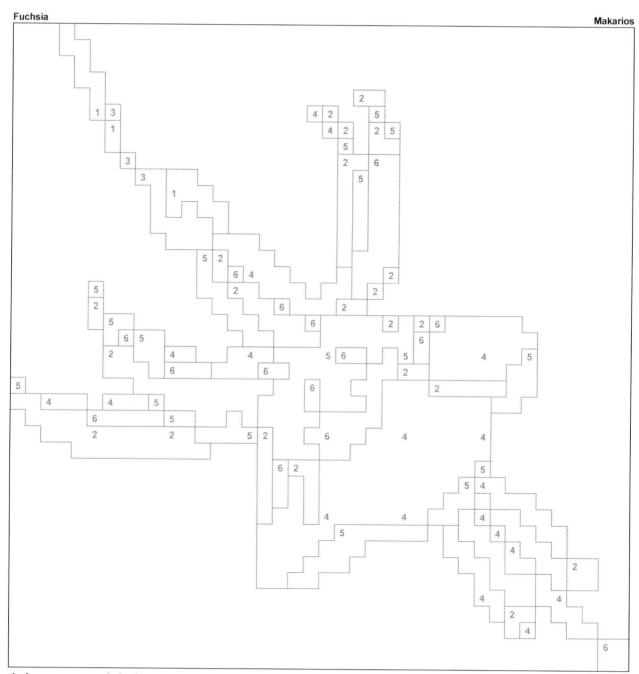

1-Asparagus, 2-Indian Red, 3-Shadow, 4-Blush, 5-Fuzzy Wuzzy, 6-Maroon

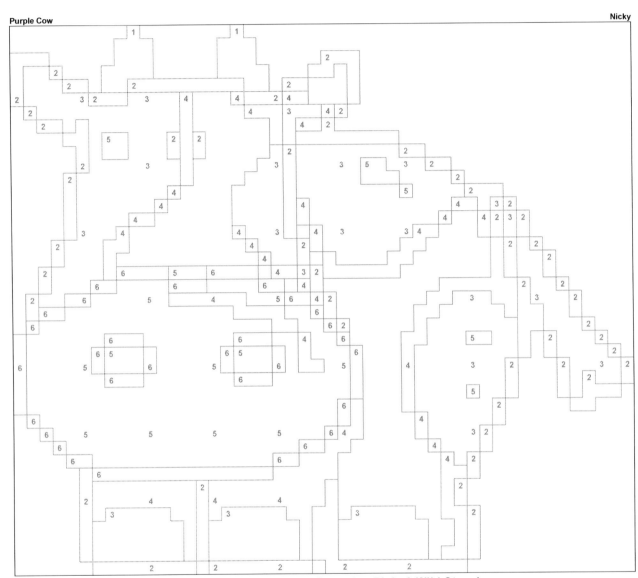

1-Mango Tango, 2-Eggplant, 3-Fuchsia, 4-Pig Pink, 5-Carnation Pink, 6-Wild Strawberry

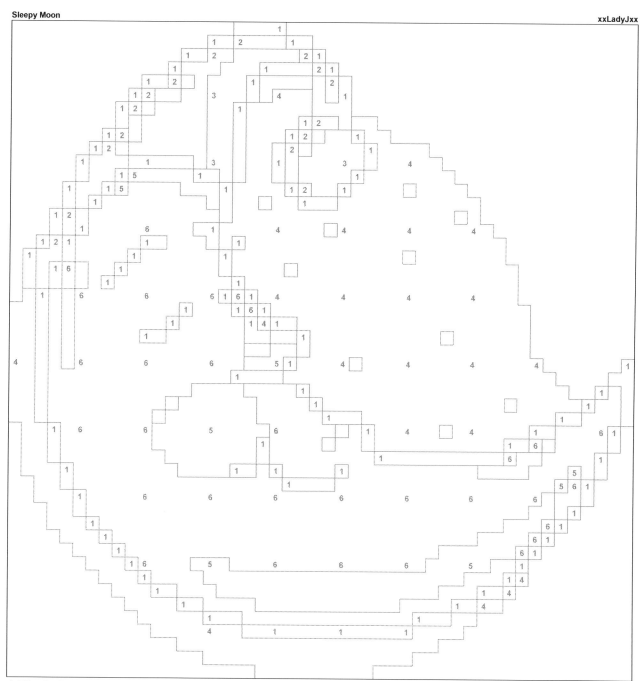

1-Black, 2-Lavender (II), 3-Orchid, 4-Pacific Blue, 5-Yellow-Orange, 6-Dandelion

Tiger Cub
llamaluva

1-Black, 2-Yellow-Orange, 3-Mango Tango, 4-Eggplant, 5-Cotton Candy

1-Outer Space, 2-Fuzzy Wuzzy, 3-Raw Sienna, 4-Green-Yellow, 5-Mango Tango, 6-Midnight Blue, 7-Wild Blue Yonder

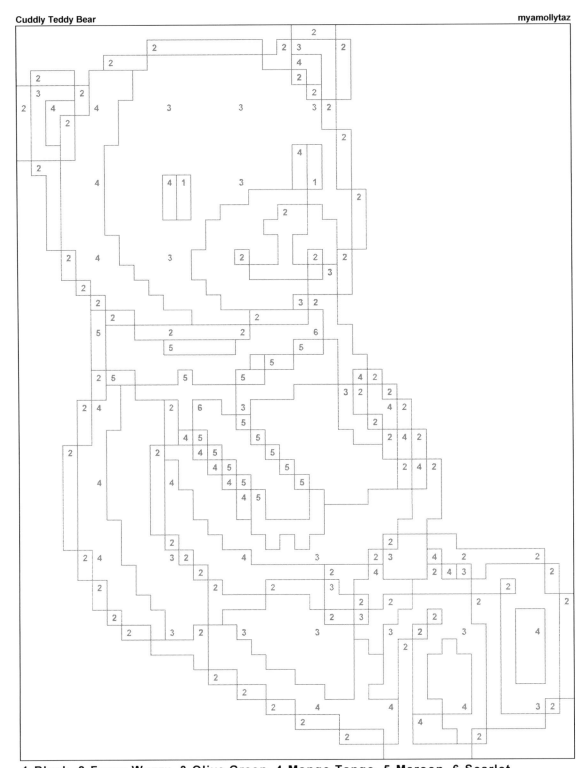

1-Black, 2-Fuzzy Wuzzy, 3-Olive Green, 4-Mango Tango, 5-Maroon, 6-Scarlet

1-Black, 2-Manatee, 3-Timberwolf, 4-Peach, 5-Fuzzy Wuzzy

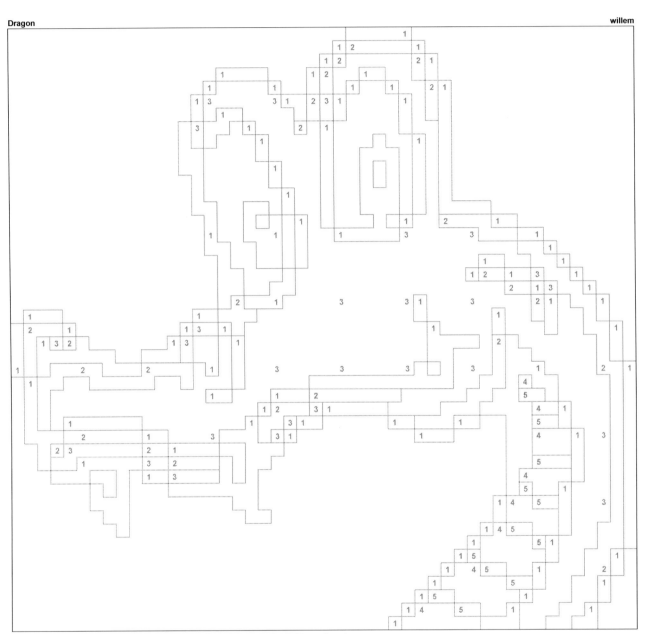

1-Black, 2-Green, 3-Inchworm, 4-Tumbleweed, 5-Eggplant

1-Fuzzy Wuzzy, 2-Yellow-Green, 3-Pig Pink, 4-Black, 5-Wild Blue Yonder

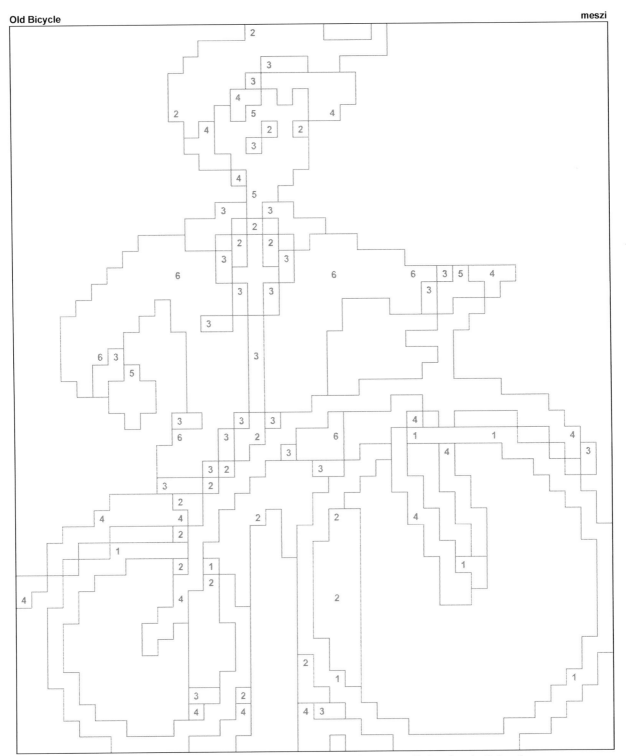

1-Fuzzy Wuzzy, 2-Blue-Violet, 3-Mango Tango, 4-Maroon, 5-Apricot, 6-Inchworm

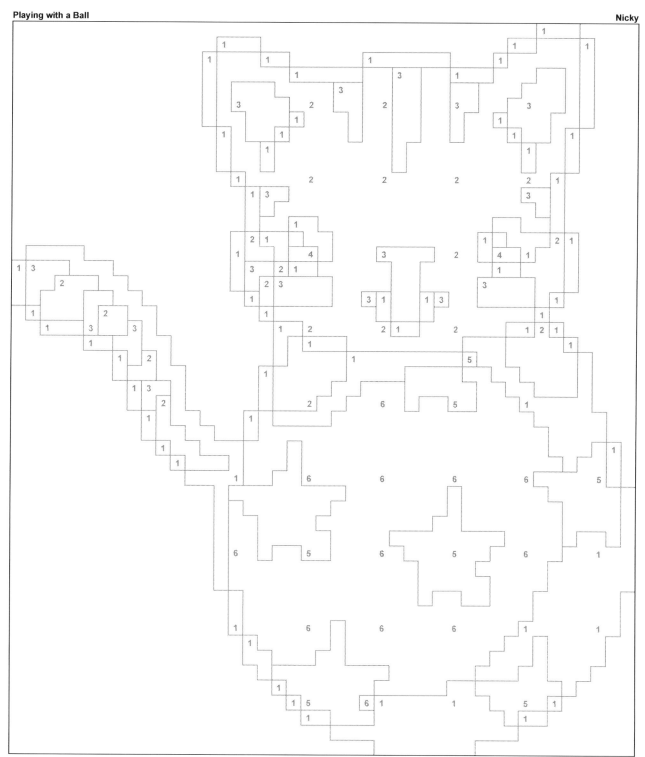

1-Wild Blue Yonder, 2-Banana Mania, 3-Tumbleweed, 4-Eggplant, 5-Goldenrod, 6-Purple
Mountains' Majesty

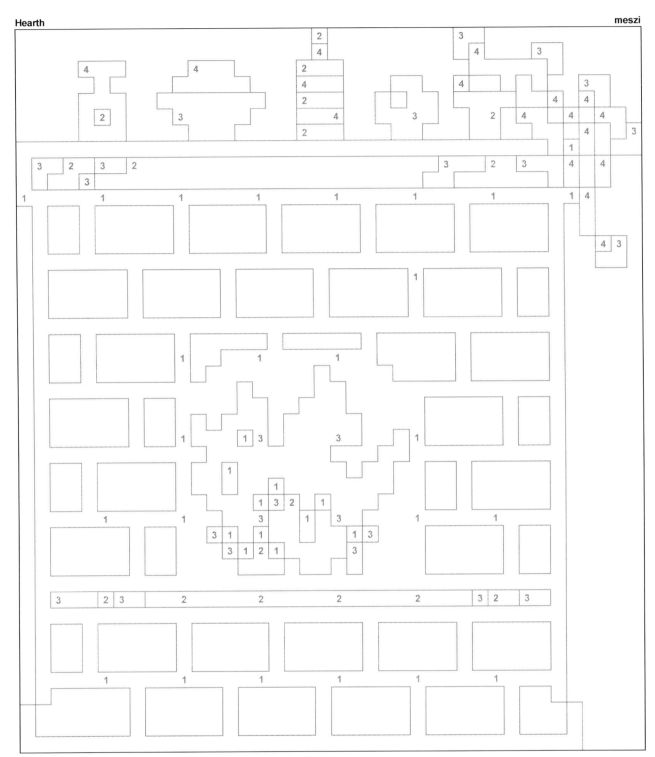

1-Black, 2-Dandelion, 3-Mango Tango, 4-Green

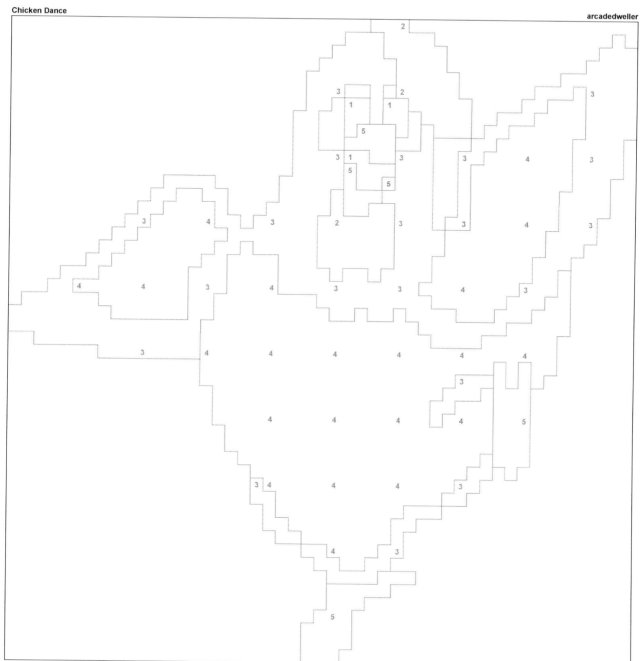

1-Black, 2-Scarlet, 3-Mango Tango, 4-Fuzzy Wuzzy, 5-Yellow-Orange

beren2005

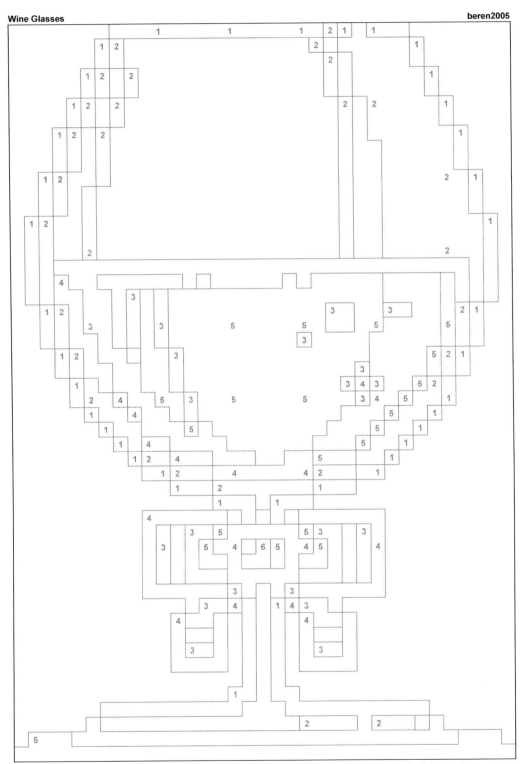

1-Blue (III), 2-Cerulean Blue, 3-Bittersweet, 4-Maroon, 5-Scarlet, 6-Dandelion

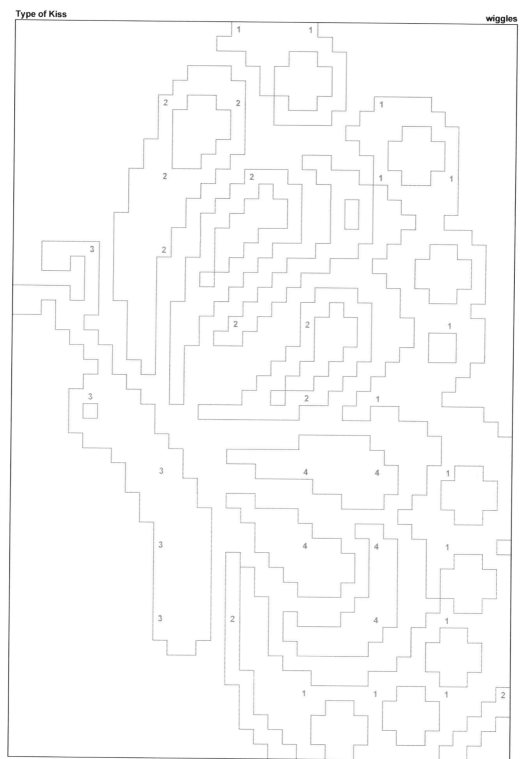

1-Wisteria, 2-Red-Violet, 3-Black, 4-Brilliant Rose

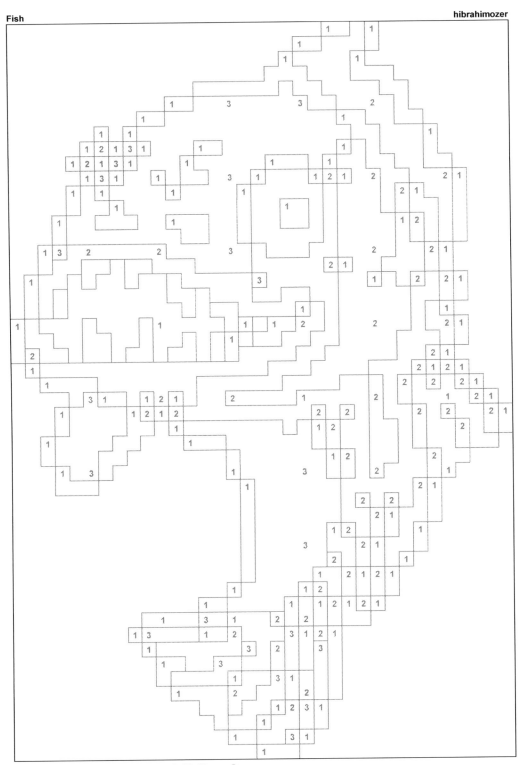

**1-Black, 2-Fuzzy Wuzzy, 3-Yellow-Orange**

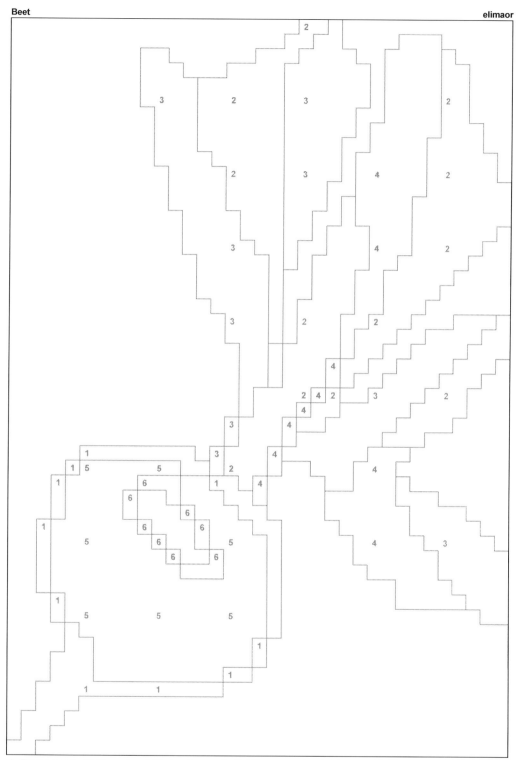

1-Eggplant, 2-Tropical Rain Forest, 3-Shamrock, 4-Green, 5-Maroon, 6-Wild S
trawberry

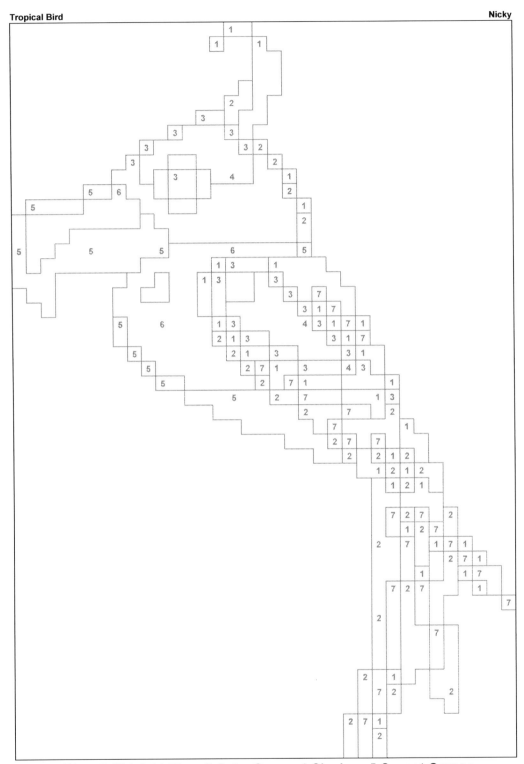

1-Navy Blue, 2-Midnight Blue, 3-Outer Space, 4-Shadow, 5-Sunset Orange,
6-Yellow-Orange, 7-Cerulean Blue

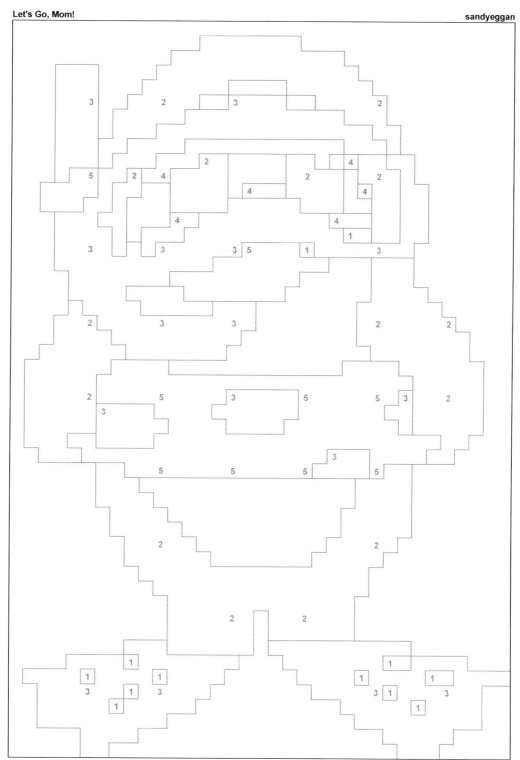

1-Shadow, 2-Black, 3-Indigo, 4-Timberwolf, 5-Dandelion

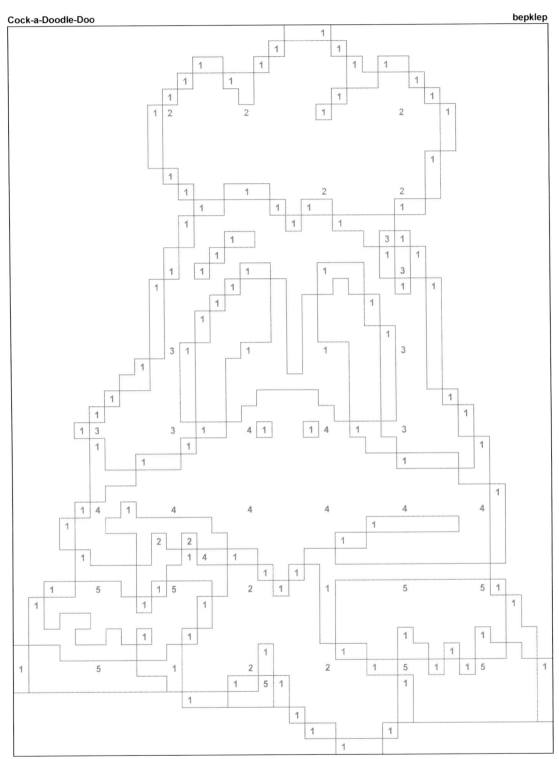

1-Black, 2-Scarlet, 3-Goldenrod, 4-Mango Tango, 5-Raw Sienna

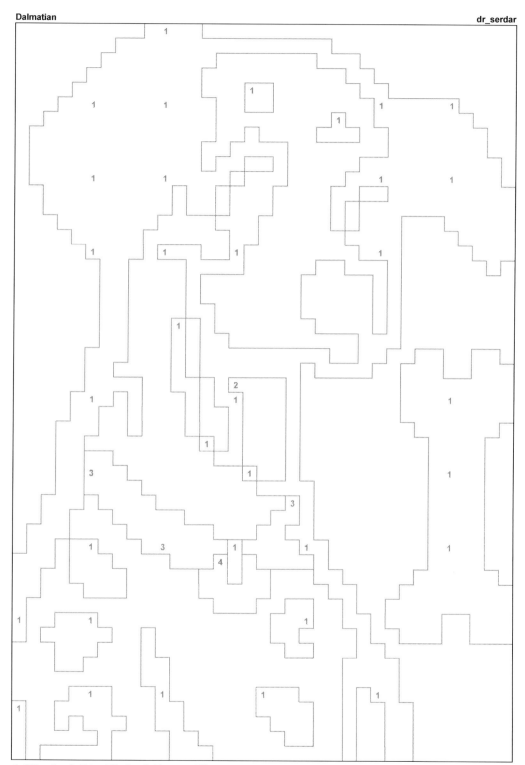

1-Black, 2-Pig Pink, 3-Fuzzy Wuzzy, 4-Dandelion

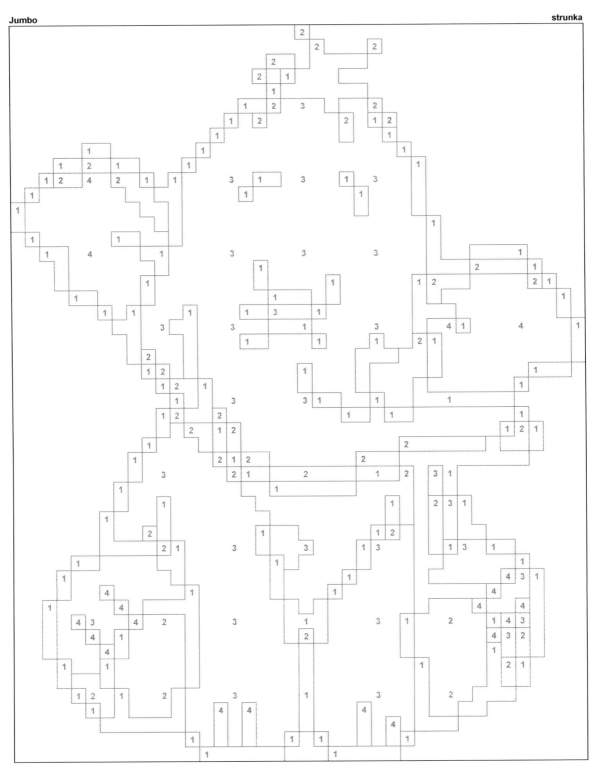

**1-Black, 2-Indigo, 3-Blue Bell, 4-Carnation Pink**

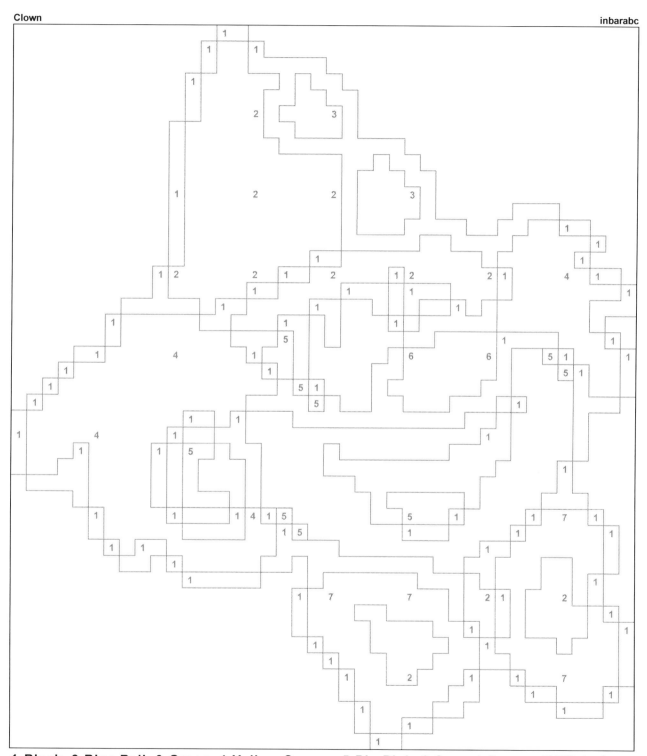

1-Black, 2-Blue Bell, 3-Green, 4-Yellow-Orange, 5-Pig Pink, 6-Sunset Orange, 7-Wisteria

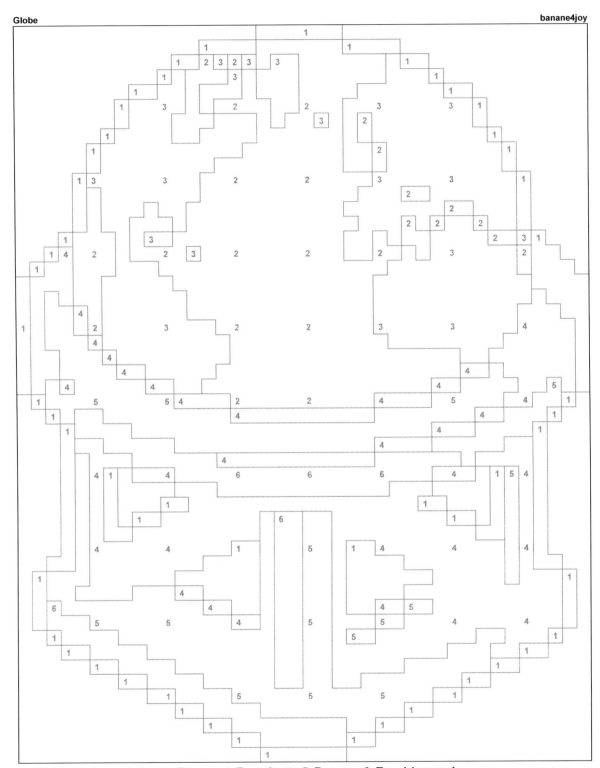

1-Black, 2-Fern, 3-Outer Space, 4-Eggplant, 5-Brown, 6-Tumbleweed

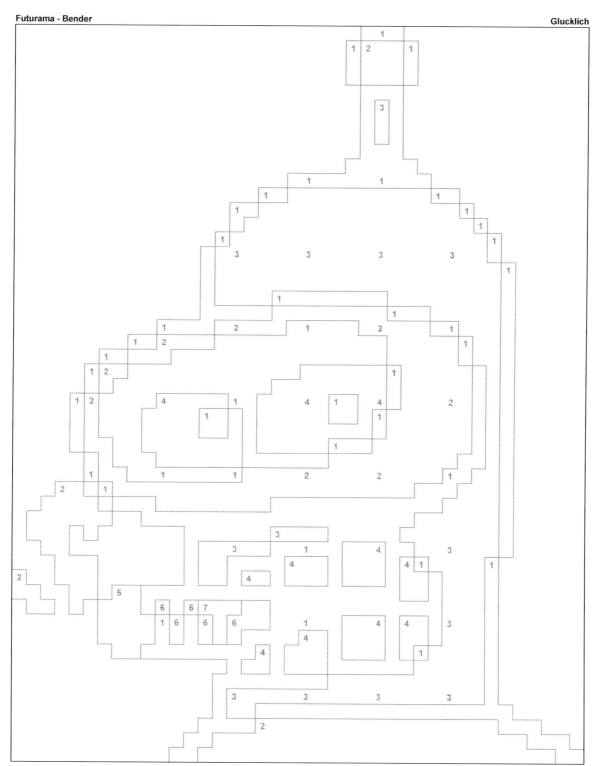

1-Black, 2-Timberwolf, 3-Cadet Blue, 4-Canary, 5-Red-Orange, 6-Fuzzy Wuzzy, 7-Yellow
-Orange

**1-Black, 2-Tropical Rain Forest, 3-Manatee, 4-Blue-Green, 5-Green**

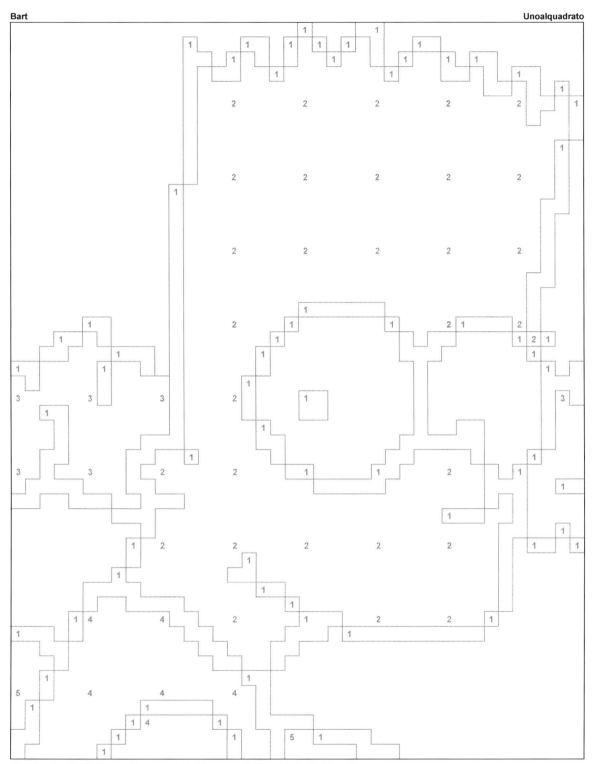

1-Black, 2-Yellow-Orange, 3-Green, 4-Scarlet, 5-Shadow

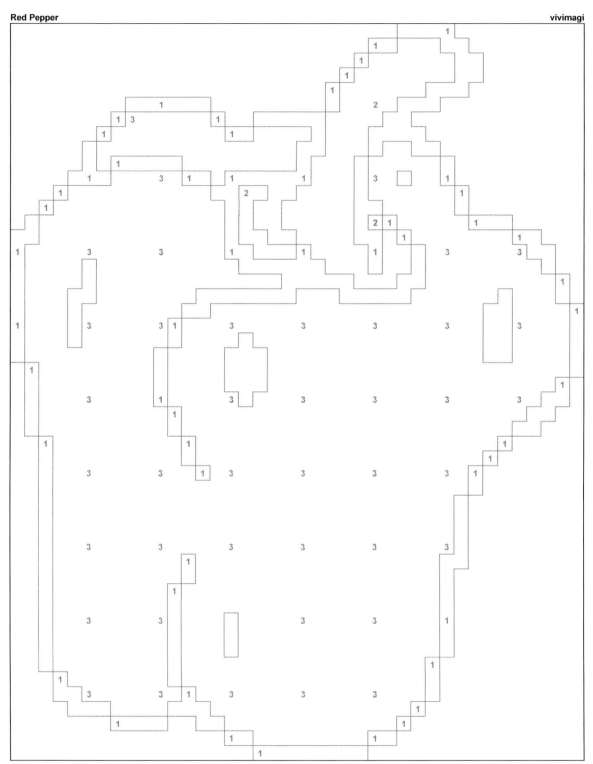

**1-Outer Space, 2-Inchworm, 3-Red-Orange**

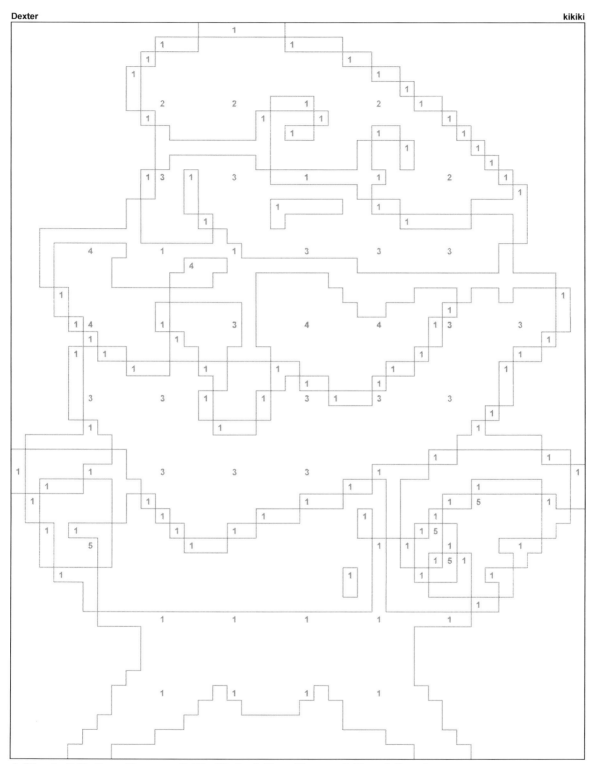

1-Black, 2-Yellow-Orange, 3-Pig Pink, 4-Cornflower, 5-Royal Purple

**1-Black, 2-Tropical Rain Forest, 3-Scarlet, 4-Yellow-Orange, 5-Blue (III)**

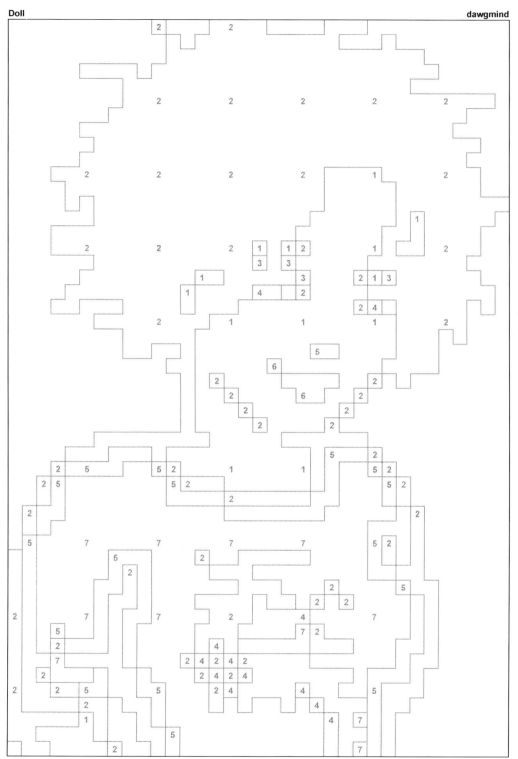

1-Tumbleweed, 2-Black, 3-Yellow, 4-Pacific Blue, 5-Blush, 6-Maroon,
7-Carnation Pink

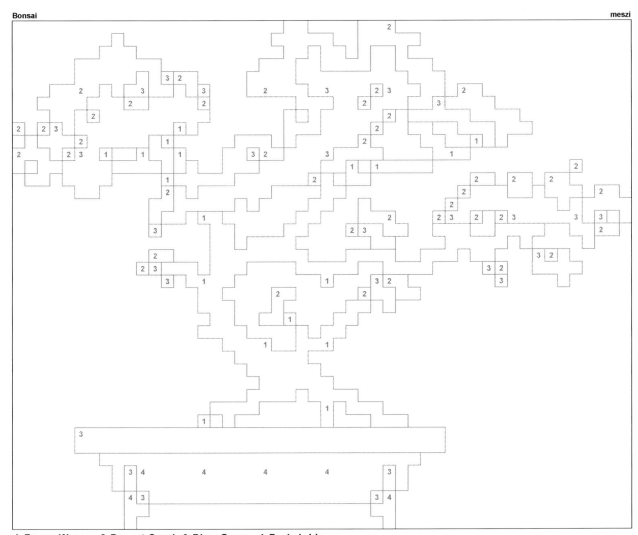

1-Fuzzy Wuzzy, 2-Desert Sand, 3-Blue-Green, 4-Periwinkle

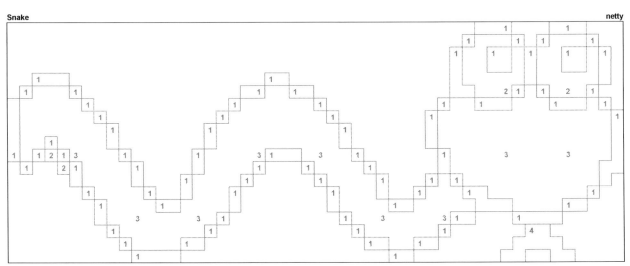

1-Black, 2-Banana Mania, 3-Green, 4-Scarlet

**1-Jungle Green, 2-Navy Blue, 3-Fuchsia, 4-Wisteria, 5-Cerulean Blue**

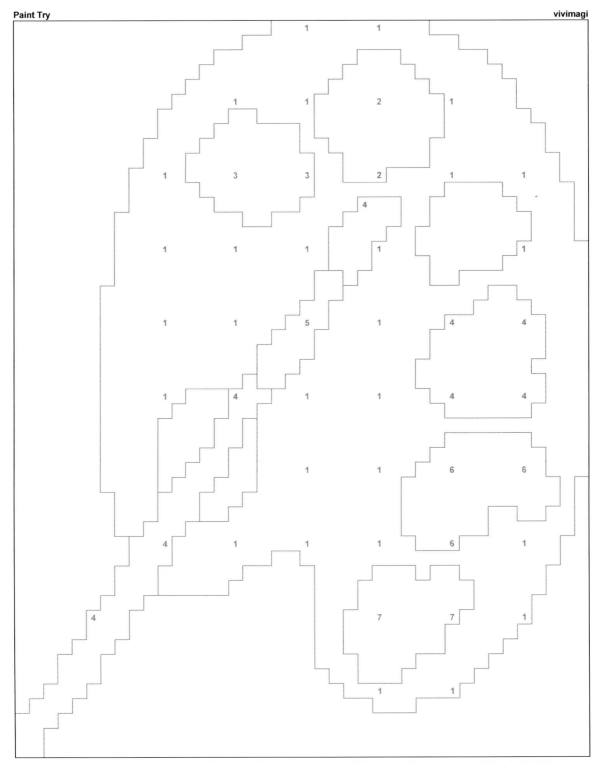

1-Tumbleweed, 2-Dandelion, 3-Tropical Rain Forest, 4-Black, 5-Manatee, 6-Midnight Blue, 7 -Scarlet

1-Mango Tango, 2-Yellow-Orange, 3-Midnight Blue, 4-Cerulean Blue, 5-Sky Blue, 6-Fuzzy
Wuzzy, 7-Blush

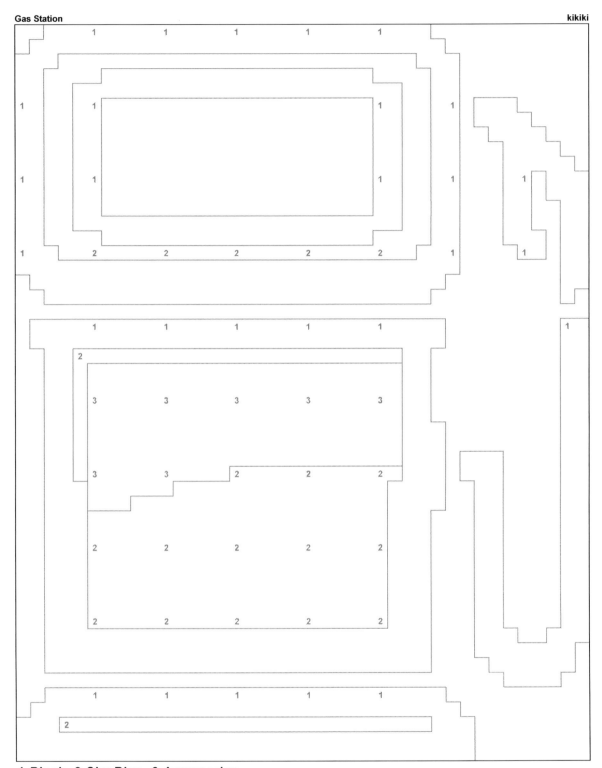

1-Black, 2-Sky Blue, 3-Aquamarine

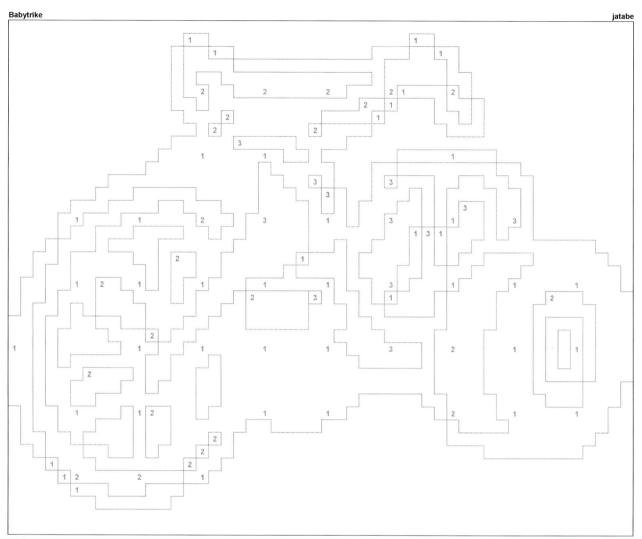

1-Outer Space, 2-Cadet Blue, 3-Jazzberry Jam

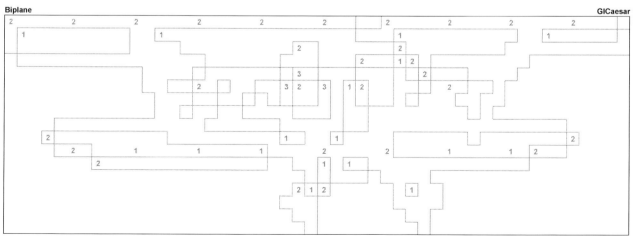

1-Outer Space, 2-Black, 3-Brick Red

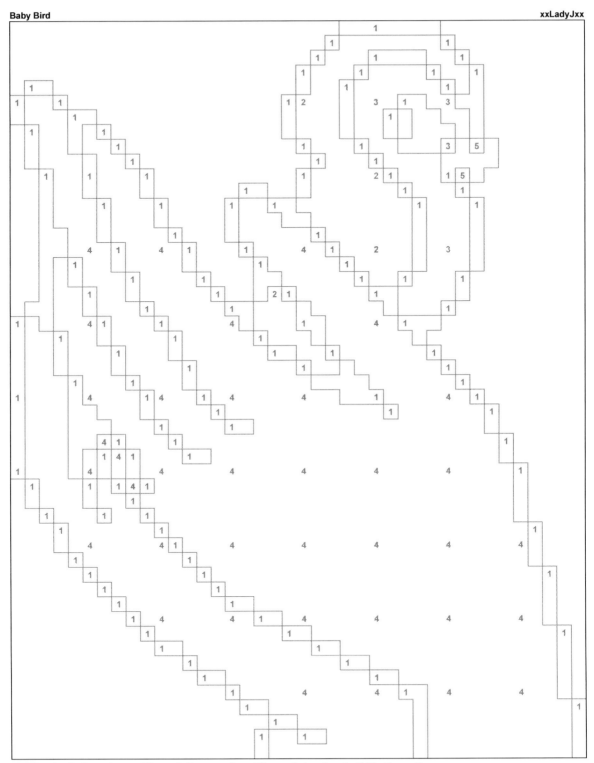

1-Black, 2-Cerulean Blue, 3-Turquoise Blue, 4-Apricot, 5-Yellow-Orange

1-Black, 2-Brown, 3-Fuzzy Wuzzy, 4-Tropical Rain Forest, 5-Dandelion

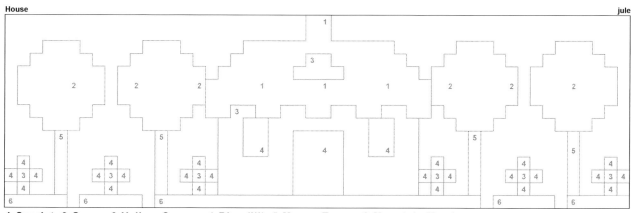

1-Scarlet, 2-Green, 3-Yellow-Orange, 4-Blue (III), 5-Mango Tango, 6-Mountain Meadow

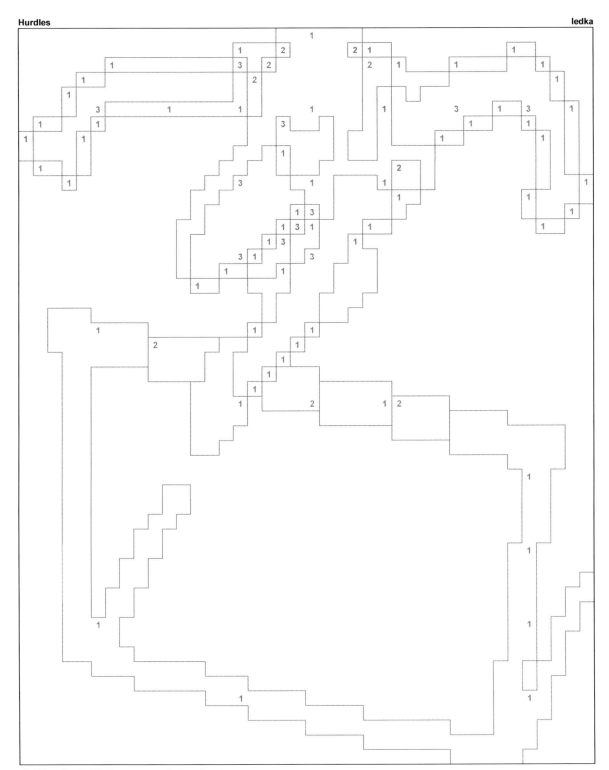

1-Black, 2-Mahogany, 3-Apricot

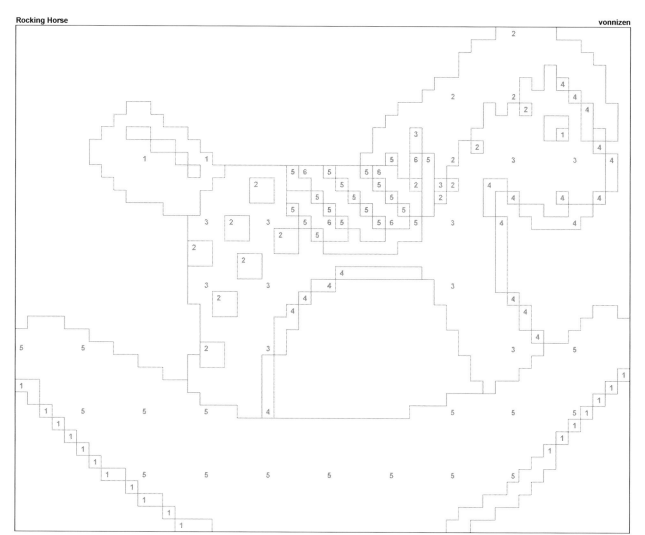

1-Black, 2-Mango Tango, 3-Sunset Orange, 4-Mahogany, 5-Green, 6-Navy Blue

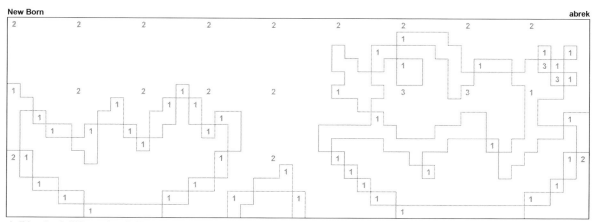

1-Black, 2-Wisteria, 3-Dandelion

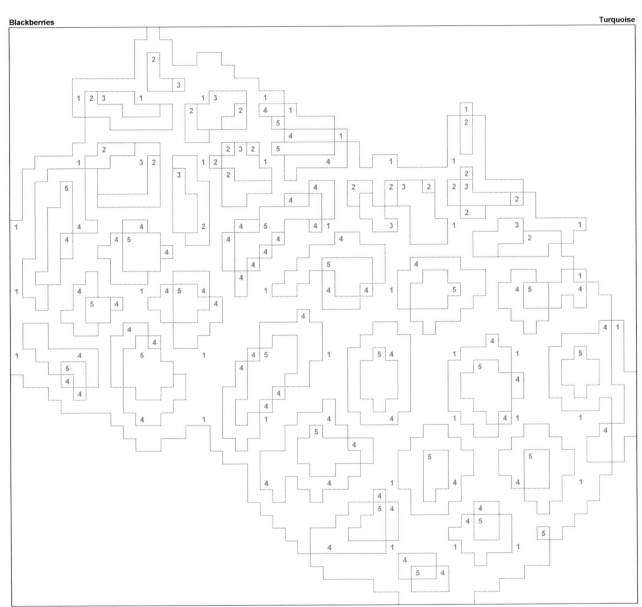

1-Black, 2-Tropical Rain Forest, 3-Green, 4-Plum, 5-Cerise

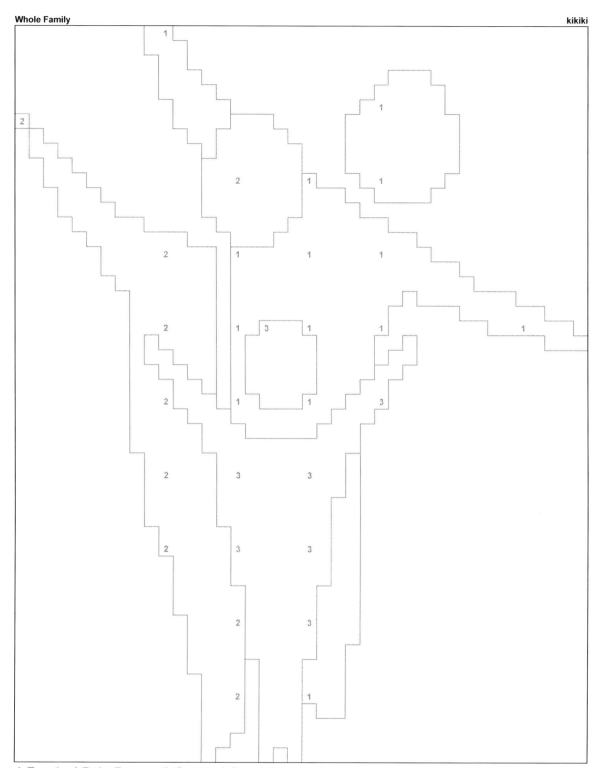

**1-Tropical Rain Forest, 2-Green, 3-Dandelion**

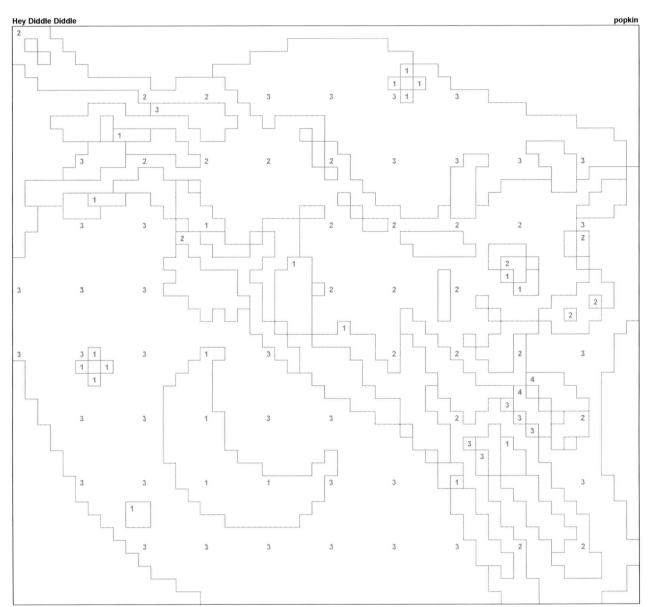

1-Canary, 2-Fuzzy Wuzzy, 3-Purple Heart, 4-Bittersweet

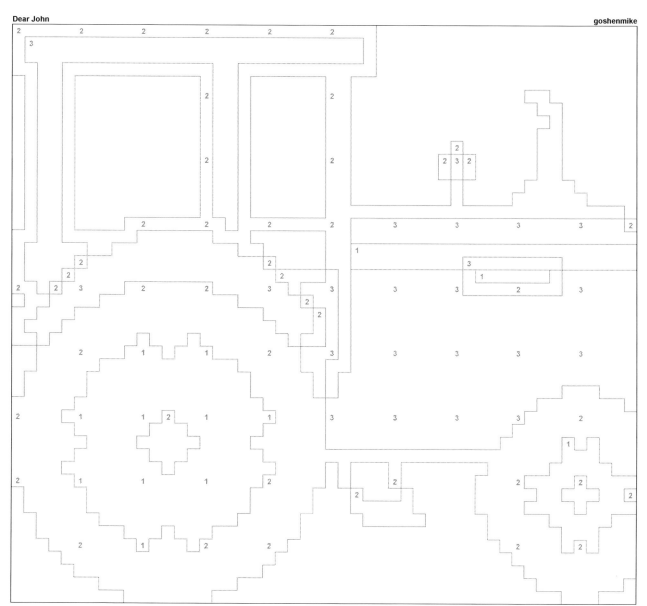

1-Yellow-Orange, 2-Black, 3-Green

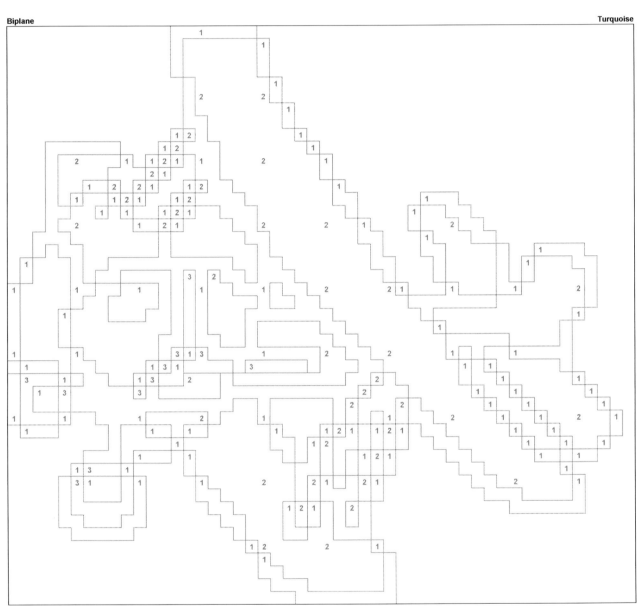

1-Black, 2-Burnt Orange, 3-Manatee

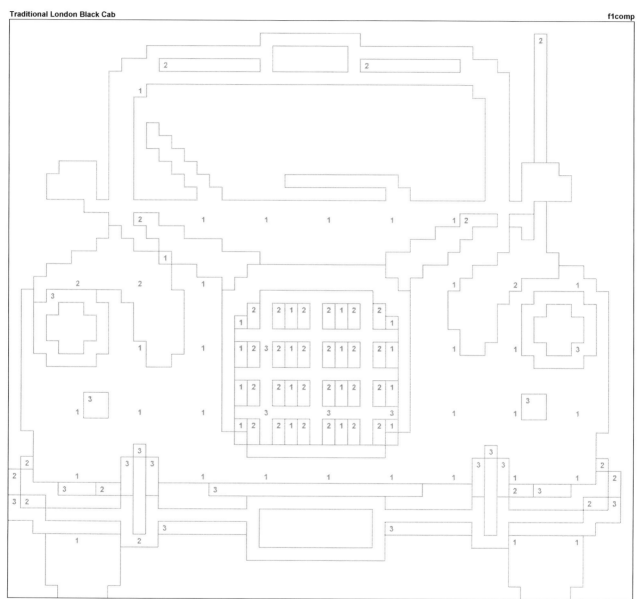

1-Black, 2-Shadow, 3-Periwinkle

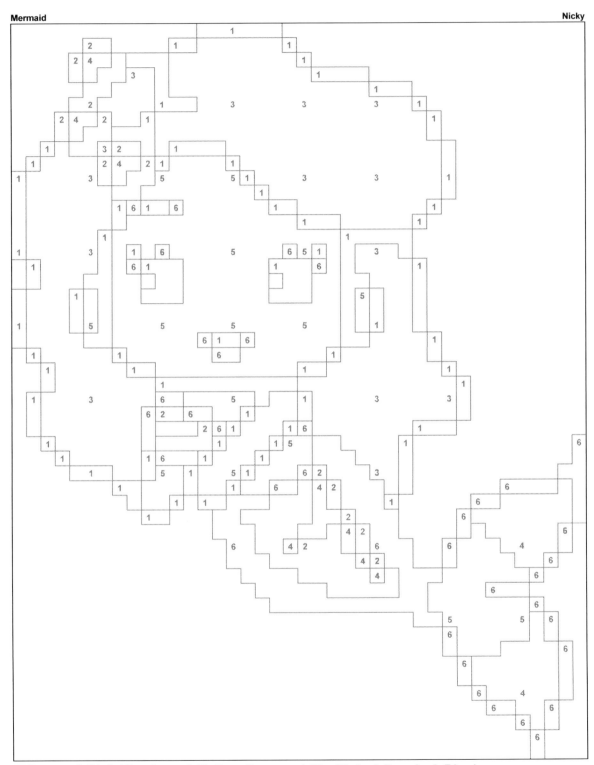

1-Brown, 2-Pink Flamingo, 3-Yellow-Orange, 4-Pig Pink, 5-Peach, 6-Blush

**1-Black, 2-Asparagus, 3-Maroon**

1-Black, 2-Bittersweet, 3-Scarlet, 4-Indian Red

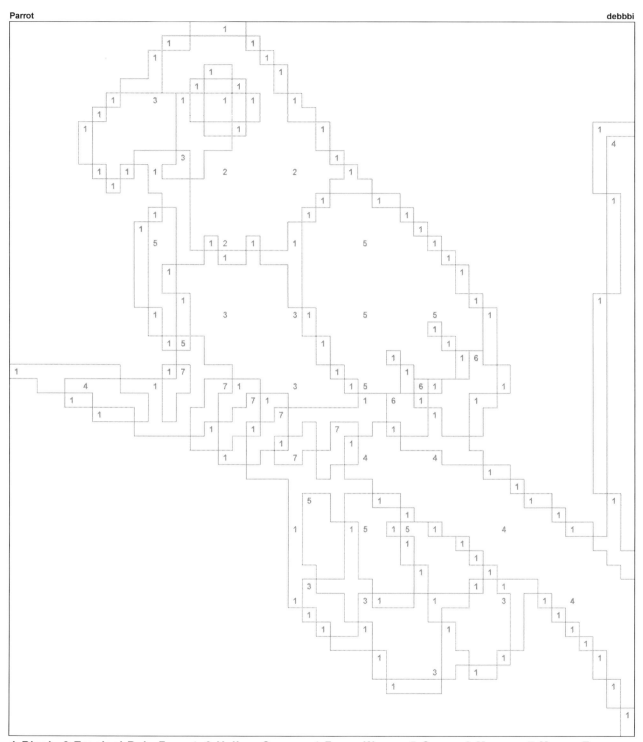

1-Black, 2-Tropical Rain Forest, 3-Yellow-Orange, 4-Fuzzy Wuzzy, 5-Green, 6-Maroon, 7-Mango Tango

1-Outer Space, 2-Cerulean Blue, 3-Robin's Egg Blue, 4-Dandelion, 5-Pig Pink, 6-Scarlet, 7-Tropical
Rain Forest

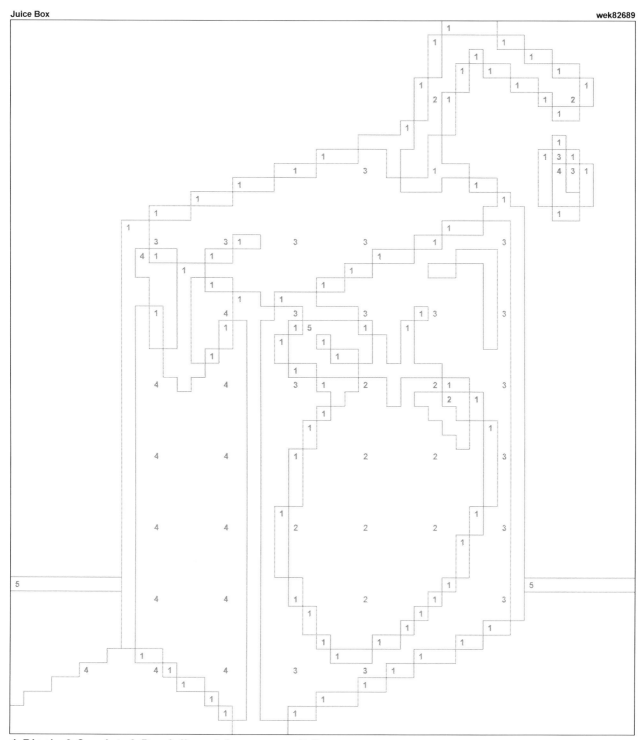

1-Black, 2-Scarlet, 3-Dandelion, 4-Asparagus, 5-Green

**Balsamic Sauce**

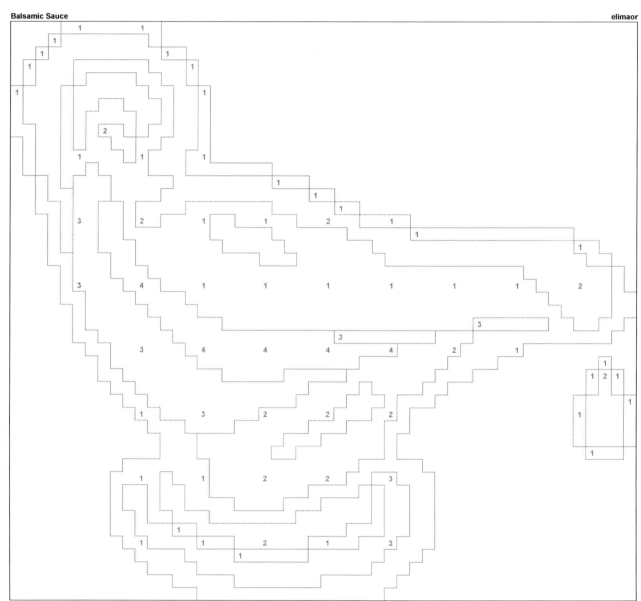

1-Black, 2-Yellow-Orange, 3-Dandelion, 4-Shadow

www.griddlers.net

**84**

**Paint by Numbers, Vol. 2**

**1-Navy Blue, 2-Periwinkle, 3-Cerulean, 4-Turquoise Blue, 5-Shadow, 6-Manatee**

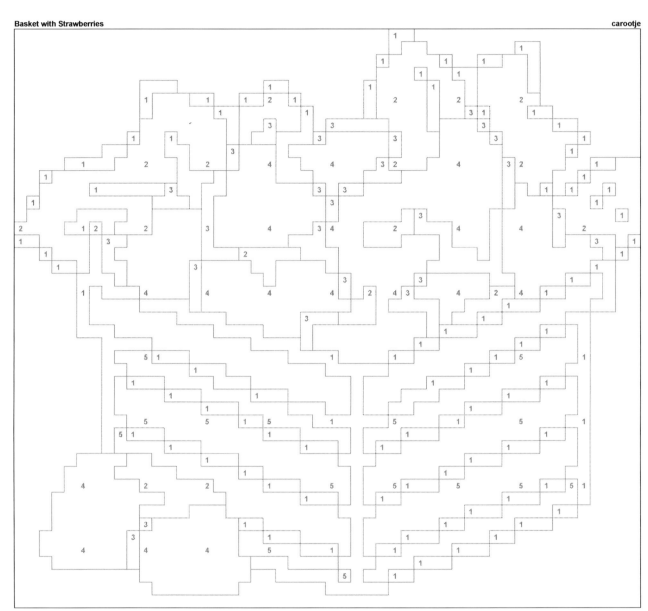

1-Outer Space, 2-Green, 3-Fuzzy Wuzzy, 4-Mahogany, 5-Yellow-Orange

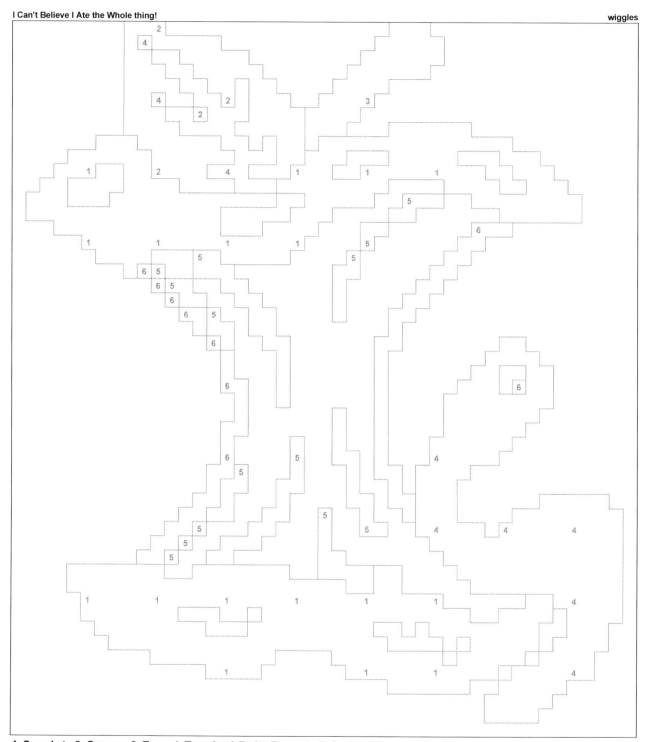

1-Scarlet, 2-Green, 3-Tan, 4-Tropical Rain Forest, 5-Cadet Blue, 6-Black

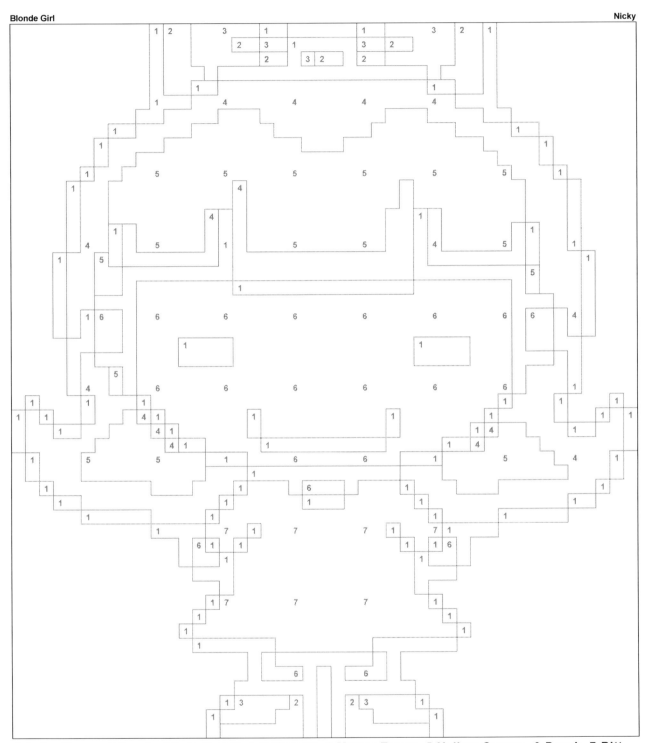

1-Outer Space, 2-Tropical Rain Forest, 3-Inchworm, 4-Mango Tango, 5-Yellow-Orange, 6-Peach, 7-Bittersweet

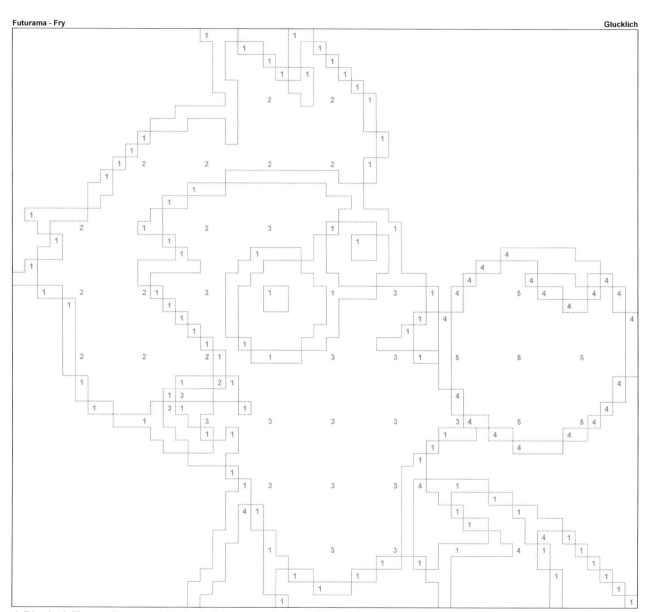

1-Black, 2-Mango Tango, 3-Apricot, 4-Maroon, 5-Carnation Pink

1-Shadow, 2-Black, 3-Asparagus, 4-Tan, 5-Wild Blue Yonder, 6-Denim

**1-Black, 2-Blue (III), 3-Manatee, 4-Dandelion, 5-Caribbean Green, 6-Tropical Rain Forest**

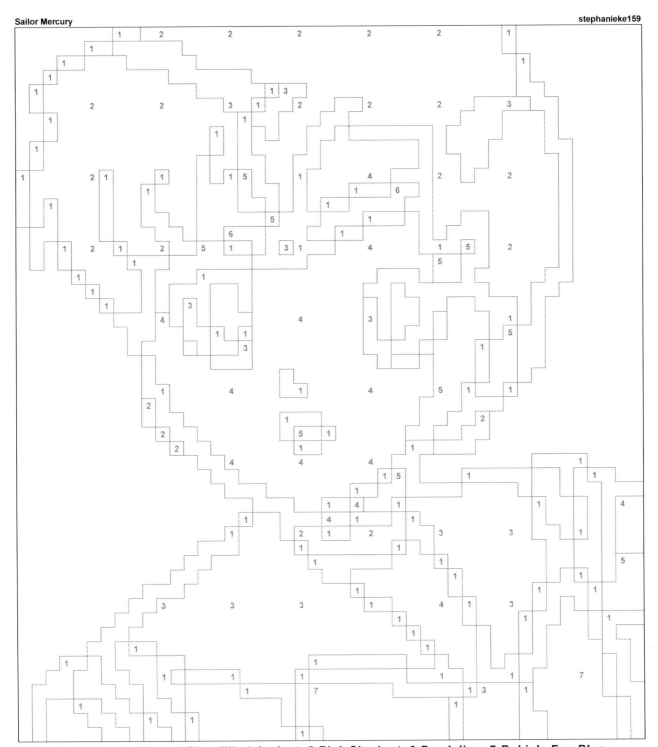

1-Black, 2-Midnight Blue, 3-Blue (III), 4-Apricot, 5-Pink Sherbert, 6-Dandelion, 7-Robin's Egg Blue

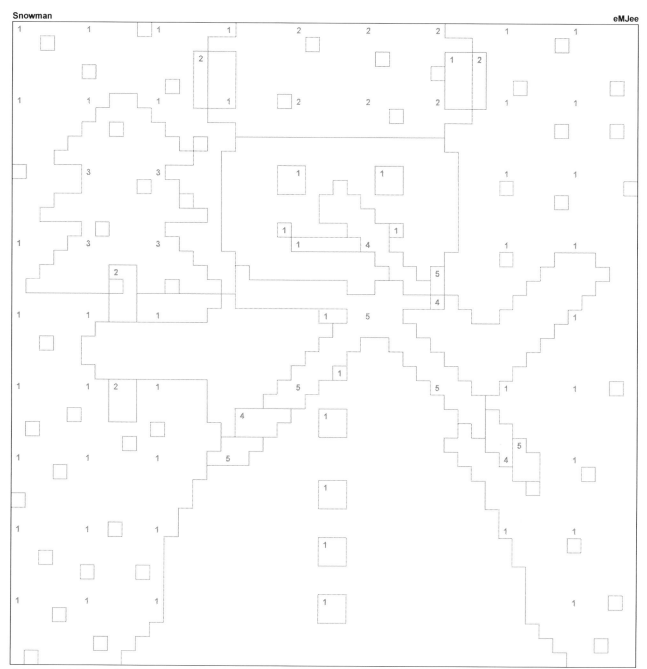

1-Black, 2-Fuzzy Wuzzy, 3-Green, 4-Scarlet, 5-Blue (III)

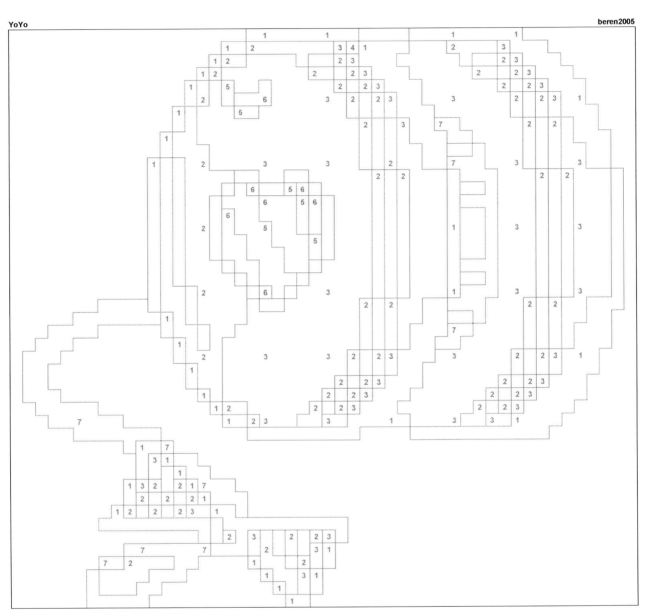

1-Razzmatazz, 2-Cotton Candy, 3-Magenta, 4-Violet-Red, 5-Yellow-Orange, 6-Dandelion, 7-Cerulean Blue

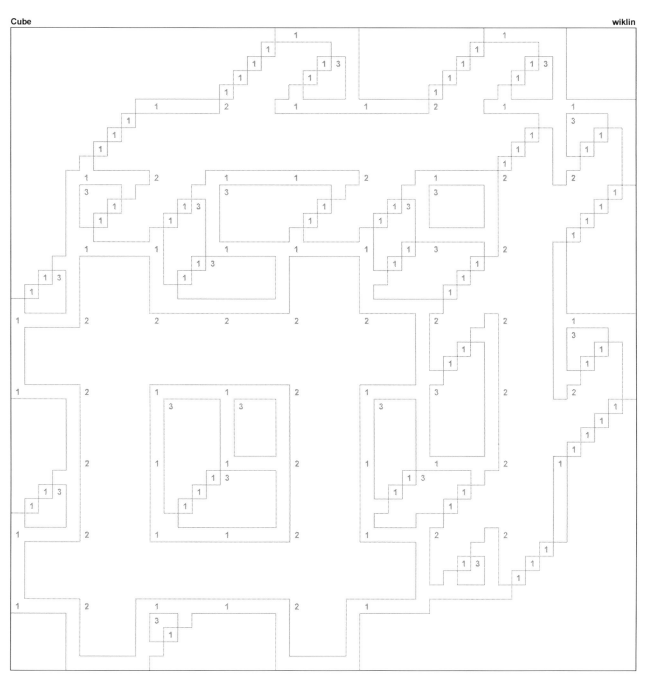

**1-Black, 2-Mango Tango, 3-Tropical Rain Forest**

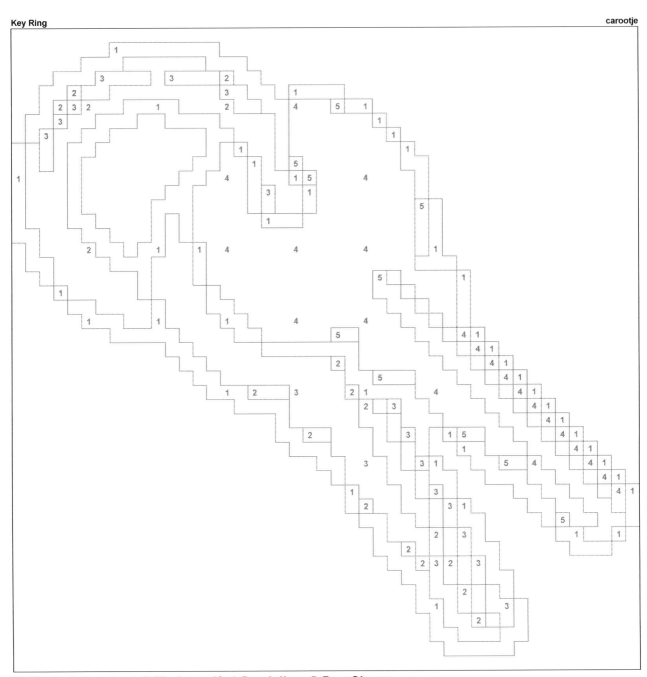

**1-Black, 2-Eggplant, 3-Timberwolf, 4-Dandelion, 5-Raw Sienna**

1-Black, 2-Spring Green, 3-Navy Blue, 4-Peach, 5-Scarlet

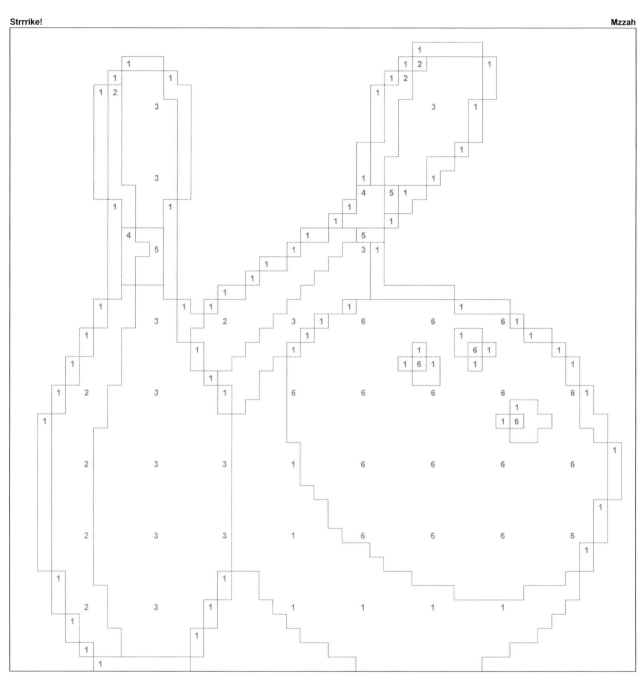

1-Black, 2-Shadow, 3-Timberwolf, 4-Maroon, 5-Scarlet, 6-Purple Heart

1-Plum, 2-Pig Pink, 3-Outer Space, 4-Black

Violin                                                                    yeu

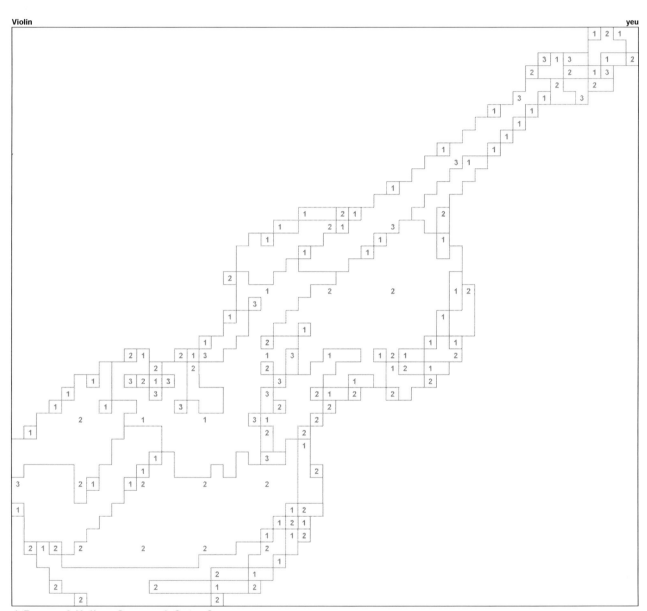

1-Brown, 2-Yellow-Orange, 3-Outer Space

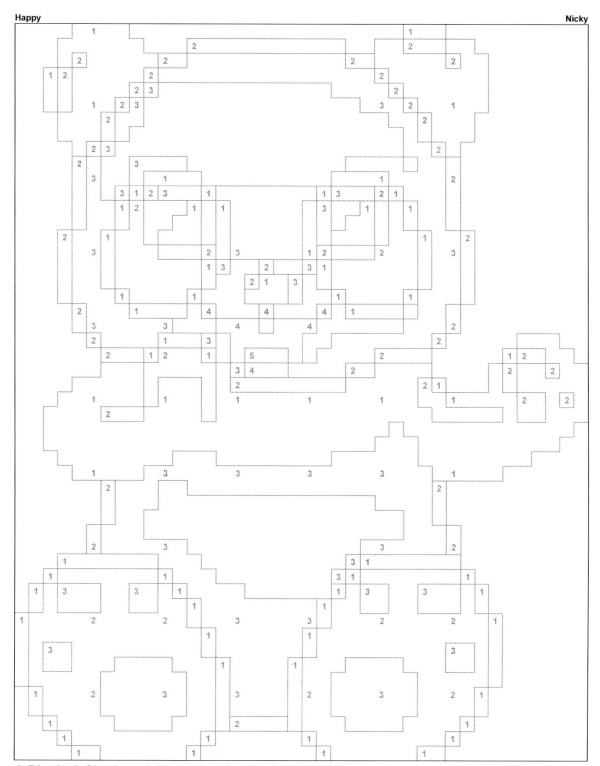

**1-Black, 2-Shadow, 3-Timberwolf, 4-Beaver, 5-Tan**

1-Maroon, 2-Black, 3-Beaver

1-Black, 2-Pig Pink, 3-Mauvelous, 4-Blush, 5-Cadet Blue

1-Asparagus, 2-Green, 3-Burnt Orange, 4-Mango Tango

1-Asparagus, 2-Granny Smith Apple, 3-Brilliant Rose, 4-Tumbleweed, 5-Brown, 6-Shadow, 7-Cadet Blue

# gRiddLERS
## Logic Puzzles

# Puzzles available in Griddlers books:

## Picture Logic Puzzles:

### Griddlers

**Griddlers** are picture logic puzzles in which cells in a grid have to be colored or left blank according to numbers given at the side of the grid to reveal a hidden picture.

### Triddlers

**Triddlers** are logic puzzles, similar to Griddlers, with the same basic rules of solving. In Triddlers the clues encircle the entire grid. The direction of the clues is horizontal, vertical, or diagonal.

### MultiGriddlers

**MultiGriddlers** are large puzzles that consist of several parts of common griddlers. A Multi can have 2 to 100 parts. The parts are bundled and, once completed, create a bigger picture.

## Word Search Puzzles:

### Word Search

**Word Search** is a word game that is letters of a word in a grid. The goal of the game is to find and mark all the words hidden inside the grid. The words may appear horizontally, vertically or diagonally, from top to bottom or bottom to top, from left to right or right to left. A list of the hidden words is provided.

Each puzzle has some text and underscores ( _ _ _ ) to indicate missing word(s). If the puzzle was solved successfully, the remaining letters pop up in the grid and the missing words appear in the text.

# Smart Things Begin With Griddlers.net

# Puzzles available in Griddlers books:

## Number Logic Puzzles:

### Sudoku

**Sudoku** is a logic-based, number-placement puzzle. The goal is to fill a grid with digits so that each column and each row contain the digits only once.

### Irregular Blocks (Jigsaws)

**Jigsaw** puzzle is played the same as Sudoku, except that the grid has Irregular Blocks, also known as cages.

### Killer Sudoku

The grid of the **Killer Sudoku** is covered by cages (groups of cells), marked with dotted outlines. Each cage encloses 2 or more cells. The top-left cell is labeled with a cage sum, which is the sum of all solution digits for the cells inside the cage.

### Kakuro

**Kakuro** is played on a grid of filled and barred cells, "black" and "white" respectively. The grid is divided into "entries" (lines of white cells) by the black cells. The black cells contain a slash from upper-left to lower-right and a number in one or both halves. These numbers are called "clues".

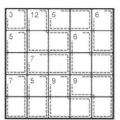

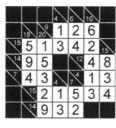

### Binary

Complete the grid with zeros (0's) and ones (1's) until there are just as many zeros and ones in every row and every column.

# Smart Things Begin With Griddlers.net

# Puzzles available in Griddlers books:

## Number Logic Puzzles:

### Greater Than / Less Than

**Greater Than** (or **Less Than**) Sudoku has no given clues (digits). Instead, there are "Greater Than" (>) or "Less Than" (<) signs between adjacent cells, which signify that the digit in one cell should be greater than or less than another.

### Futoshiki

**Futoshiki** is played on a grid that may show some digits at the start. Additionally, there are "Greater Than" (>) or "Less Than" (<) signs between adjacent cells, which signify that the digit in one cell should be greater than or less than another.

### Kalkudoku

The grid of the **Kalkudoku** is divided into heavily outlined cages (groups of cells). The numbers in the cells of each cage must produce a certain "target" number when combined using a specified mathematical operation (either addition, subtraction, multiplication or division).

### Straights

**Straights** (**Str8ts**) is played on a grid that is partially divided by black cells into compartments. Compartments must contain a straight - a set of consecutive numbers - but in any order (for example: 2-1-3-4). There can also be white clues in black cells.

### Skyscrapers

The **Skyscrapers** puzzle has numbers along the edge of the grid. Those numbers indicate the number of buildings which you would see from that direction if there was a series of skyscrapers with heights equal the entries in that row or column.

Made in the USA
Middletown, DE
10 August 2017